P9-DID-112

ATLANTIC HISTORY

ATLANTIC HISTORY
Concept and Contours

————

Bernard Bailyn

HARVARD UNIVERSITY PRESS

Cambridge, Massachusetts

London, England

2005

Library of Congress Cataloging-in-Publication Data

Bailyn, Bernard.
Atlantic history / Bernard Bailyn.
p. cm.
Includes bibliographical references and index.
ISBN 0-674-01688-2 (alk. paper)
1. Atlantic Ocean Region—Historiography.   I. Title.
D13.5.A75B35 2005
909'.09821'0072—dc22   2004059696

For the members of the
Atlantic History Seminar

Contents

Preface

HISTORY is what has happened, in act and thought; it is also what historians make of it. This book is about both, as they relate to a very large subject now coming into focus. It is an effort to trace the emergence of historians' awareness and the nature of the subject itself. In the whole of such a large field, no one, least of all myself, is expert in all the areas involved. In some I have much experience, in others I have very little, and defer to the authorities. But the effort, whatever the limitations, is to sketch both aspects of the subject, and thereby, in some small degree, enlarge the discourse of this passage of Western history.

I

The Idea of Atlantic History

ATLANTIC HISTORY—from the first encounters of Europeans with the Western Hemisphere through the Revolutionary era—is a subject that certain historians have found strange, that others have said does not exist and if it does exist it shouldn't, that at best has no easy or clear definition, and that yet in recent years has emerged in college and university teaching programs across the United States and is taught elsewhere as well—in Galway, Ireland; in Dundee, Scotland; in Liverpool, Sydney, Vienna, and Hamburg. Teaching opportunities in American colleges and universities specify Atlantic history as a desired specialty. The American Historical Association has a prize for books in Atlantic history. There have been international conferences on the subject in Hamburg, Leiden, Glasgow, and Williamsburg. Harvard University has held an annual seminar on the subject for young historians drawn from the four Atlantic continents as part of a project that includes workshops, a website, and publications. Papers on Atlantic history have been presented at academic conventions and appear in journals as different as the Dutch *Itin-erario* and the French *Dix-Huitième Siècle*.[1]

How this came about, the emergence of this interest in Atlantic history as more than a geographical expression—as a subject itself, as a historical conception, as an essential passage in the development of the world we know—has its own history. It is a story that winds through the public life of the late twentieth century, through the interior impulses of technical scholarship, and through the social situation of those who write history. It arose neither from the wholly disengaged contemplation of the past nor from the anachronistic back-projection of the present. A deeply embedded part of early modern history, it is peculiarly relevant for understanding the present. And its origins and development may illustrate something of the general process by which covering ideas in historical study, framing notions, emerge, and something of the forces that impel and shape them.

I

How had the idea of Atlantic history developed? Not in imitation of Fernand Braudel's concept of Mediterranean history, despite the fact that French "Atlanticists" like Pierre Chaunu have ritually invoked Braudel's name and the inspiration of his famous book. For Braudel's *The Mediterranean and the Mediterranean World in the Age of Philip II* is *dis*aggregative—taking apart in three dimensions of time, not putting together, the elements of a world. It is conceptually meta-historical not historical, based on a formulation essentially epistemological not historical. And the impulse behind it, as Braudel himself said, was essentially "poetic," a reflection of his personal engagement with, his love of the Mediterranean world.

Nor is it simply an expansion of the venerable tradition of "imperial" history, either British, Spanish, Portuguese, or Dutch, though that tradition, immensely innovative in its time, was, and is, by definition at least transatlantic. Both of the leading American historians in this tradition, Charles M. Andrews and Clarence Haring, wrote works of great scope, detailing the structure and management of the British and Spanish Atlantic empires in the *ancien régime;* and both were immensely creative archival scholars. Andrews in effect discovered the Anglo-American archives of the first British empire in London's Public Record Office, catalogued them, indexed them, and put them to use, a task further developed by his most accomplished students. Haring similarly uncovered and made initial use of archives in Madrid and Seville. But neither thought of themselves as dealing with Atlantic history as such—neither used the term. They were describing the formal structure of imperial governments, not the lives of the people who lived within these governments, and they concentrated on the affairs of single nations.

Nor does "Atlantic history" emerge from the many writings, generations of writings, on exploration and discovery, works by S. E. Morison, William Hovgaard, Fridtjof Nansen, Henry Harisse, C. R. Boxer, Bailey Diffie, Edgar Prestage, J. P. Oliveira Martins, Henry

Vignaud, Antonio Pigafetta, and H. P. Biggar, followed by
a whole library of narratives of the first settlements that
resulted from the discoveries they traced. They were detailing how a world new to Europeans was gradually explored, not what the emerging world was like.

By World War II both imperial history and the history of exploration and discovery had matured as subjects,
were largely consolidated, and seemed to invite only in-
cremental contributions to a well-sketched scene, not the
exploration of a new kind of understanding. There were
institutions, laws, revolutions, and vivid tales of discovery,
but no societies or social organizations, no sustained cultural encounters. Above all, there were no large unan-
swered questions other than those that simply required
more information. There was no integration of the themes
that existed, no concept that would give the details some
general significance. There seemed to be only discrete accounts of certain elements in a large story.

Then, during and just after World War II the situation
began to change. The origin of the change is important;
it suggests a general characteristic of historiographical
movements. In part, though only in part, the initial impulses lay not within historical study but outside it, in the
public world that formed the external context of historians' awareness. The ultimate source may be traced back to
1917 and the writings of the twenty-seven-year-old Walter
Lippmann, then an avid interventionist in the European
war and already an extremely influential journalist. In *The
New Republic* in February 1917—"in one of the most im-

portant editorials he ever wrote"—he declared that America's interests in the European war lay with the Allies, and that the country was driven to intervene not merely to protect "the Atlantic highway" but to preserve the

> profound web of interest which joins together the western world. Britain, France, Italy, even Spain, Belgium, Holland, the Scandinavian nations, and Pan-America are in the main one community in their deepest needs and their deepest purposes . . . We cannot betray the Atlantic community by submitting . . . What we must fight for is the common interest of the western world, for the integrity of the Atlantic Powers. We must recognize that we are in fact one great community and act as members of it.

Two months later he was vindicated when the United States entered the war.[2]

But Lippmann's hopes for a formal, enduring construction of an Atlantic community faded in the isolationist aftermath of the war and disappeared in the domestic turmoil of the Depression. His views of 1917 were not forgotten, however, and during World War II they were recovered in another struggle over intervention, first by Forrest Davis and then by Lippmann himself.

Davis, a fellow journalist, published in 1941 *The Atlantic System,* a book-length commentary on Roosevelt and Churchill's "Atlantic Charter," in which he reviewed the history of Anglo-American relations and quoted Lippmann at length to argue the case for intervention. The book was a fervent political tract, denouncing "the Axis blueprints for a New World Order [as] a sterile prison-house inhabited by robotlike heroes and faceless subject races" and arguing that "The Atlantic System is old, rational, and pragmatic. Growing organically out of strategic and political realities in a congenially free climate, its roots run deep and strong into the American tradition."[3] Two years later Lippmann resumed his arguments of 1917, adapting them in sharpened form to the problem of the world order that would follow the end of the war. In his *U.S. War Aims*, written in 1943 but delayed in publication until, a month after D-Day, the outcome of the war seemed assured, Lippmann argued that the new postwar world order would, and should, be dominated by "great regional constellations of states which are homelands, not of one nation alone but of the historic civilized communities." First among them, he wrote, will or should be the Atlantic Community, which was, he said, an "oceanic system" whose chief military powers were, in respect to one another, islands. There were of course national differences within the Atlantic region, but they were "variations within the same cultural tradition," which was "the extension of Western or Latin Christendom from the Western Mediterranean into the whole basin of the Atlantic Ocean."[4]

Though Lippmann drew on a general sense of history, his book, like Davis's, was a political tract, a program of *Realpolitik* that abandoned Wilsonian universalism and One World idealism in favor of the protection of national self-interest. His view of the postwar world as a cluster of regional power centers dominated by the Atlantic states was picked up by other commentators and politicians and played into the developing confrontational world order that followed the end of the war. The decade after 1945 saw the creation of the Marshall Plan, the Truman Doctrine, and the North Atlantic Treaty Organization; and it saw too the emergence of a plethora of overlapping nongovernmental organizations throughout the Western world in support of the Atlantic Alliance. With divisive pressures building up in France and Britain, with conflicts within the American establishment on which way to turn in foreign policy, and with the constant danger of a revived isolationism, the need for consolidation was obvious. In 1961 the three main groups in America—the Atlantic Council, the American Committee for the Atlantic Institute, the American Council on NATO—joined together with other groups to form, under the leadership of former secretaries of state Christian Herter and Dean Acheson, the Atlantic Council of the United States. Its honorary chairmen were former presidents Hoover, Truman, and Eisenhower, and its purpose was "to act as an educational medium to stimulate thought and discussion with respect to the need and problems of developing greater Atlantic unity." Made up of "prominent individuals who are themselves convinced of the pivotal importance of Atlantic cooperation in promoting the strength of the free world," the Council reached out to the public in every way it could, in book and pamphlet publications, in speeches and conferences, and especially, starting in 1963, in a new journal, *The Atlantic Community Quarterly*.

The *Quarterly* was founded, the editors wrote, "on the premise that something new is being born in the world today." Once men seeking better ways to organize their existence invented city-states, then nation-states, and now "something larger is being born. The Atlantic Community, tying together . . . nations on both sides of the Atlantic Ocean, has already reached a state of spirited dialogue." The *Quarterly*'s aim, it informed its readers, was "to monitor the entire Atlantic Community for you and to bring you the best of this dialogue from wherever it might appear." It professed no single point of view other than the conviction "that the Atlantic Community is a historic inevitability and that somehow . . . a true Atlantic Community will come into being during the lifetime of most of us."

The *Quarterly* did indeed monitor the Atlantic Community. In issue after issue it published or republished speeches, documents, debates, and transcripts of press conferences from all over Europe, Africa, and the Americas, with contributions from the entire pan-Atlantic power elite—top government officials, military leaders, bankers, corporate executives, journalists, leading academics, public intellectuals, and opinion leaders of all kinds. Among the sixty-two contributions to the first four issues were speeches and essays by former secretary of state Herter, Lord Franks (former ambassador to the

United States and chairman of Lloyds Bank), Lester Pearson (prime minister of Canada), Ludwig Erhard (German chancellor), Gerhard Schröder (German foreign minister), Halvard Lange (foreign minister of Norway), Paul-Henri Spaak (Belgian foreign minister, former prime minister, former secretary-general of NATO, and president of the UN Assembly), General de Gaulle, Valéry Giscard d'Estaing, Lyndon Johnson, John F. Kennedy, Dean Acheson, Senators Fulbright and Javits, Baron René Boel (Belgian representative at the Bretton Woods Conference), Altiero Spinelli (founder of the Federation Movement in Italy), the editor of the Swiss *Neue Zurcher Zeitung,* the editor of *Die Zeit,* Walter Lippmann, Raymond Aron (Sorbonne), and Max Beloff (Oxford). And among twenty-four documents published in the first year were the Declaration on a United Europe, excerpts from press conferences of Kennedy and de Gaulle, a Papal Encyclical, a Declaration of Atlantic Unity, and a joint U.S.-Spanish Statement.

The *Quarterly*'s immediate audience was small—2,000–5,000 subscribers—but its importance as a reflection of the international effort at the highest level to promote the idea of an historic, "inevitable" Atlantic Community and to assist in its realization was significant. And the Council's efforts went further, into promoting programs on Atlantic studies in American colleges and universities, to make certain that the "successor generation" of leaders was similarly devoted to the idea of the Atlantic Community.[5]

The public world, in the United States and elsewhere,

was thus constantly informed of the Atlanticists' views. They permeated the public atmosphere, and they were both shared and reinforced by the more politically aware historians.

The first of the professional historians to respond to these public issues were those most sensitive to the need to protect Christianity—the Christianity of the West— against the threat of Communist expansion. The most outspoken were two leading Catholic historians, who clearly grasped the relevance for historical study of the Atlanticists' underlying assumptions and implications.

In March 1945 Ross Hoffman, professor of history at Fordham University, published a broad-ranging essay entitled "Europe and the Atlantic Community." In it he stated—quoting Salvador de Madariaga of Spain and Antonio Salazar of Portugal as well as Lippmann—that the Atlantic Ocean was "the inland sea of Western Civilization," and that the "Atlantic community" ("the mighty geographic, historical and political reality that surrounds us on all sides") was "the progeny of Western Christendom."[6] That theme was fully orchestrated later that year in a notable speech by the president of the American Historical Association, Carlton J. H. Hayes of Columbia University.

Hayes, an eminent scholar, a renowned and influential teacher at Columbia University, like Hoffman a convert to Catholicism and a fervent anti-communist from the moment the wartime alliance with Russia ended, further developed the idea that there was a distinct "European or

'Western' culture" which was rooted in a common inheritance of Greco-Roman, Judeo-Christian traditions. Recently returned from a controversial ambassadorship to Spain, Hayes, in his presidential address, "The American Frontier—Frontier of What?" attacked the parochialism of American historians and their exaggerated sense of American exceptionalism, and urged them to think in terms of America's historic affiliation with Europe, now threatened by alien doctrines encroaching from the east.

> The area of this common Western culture centers in the Atlantic and extends eastward far into Europe and along African shores, from Norway and Finland to Cape Town, and westward across all America, from Canada to Patagonia.

Decrying the tradition of American cultural as well as political isolationism, warning against the equal dangers of an artificial pan-American myopia and "starry-eyed universalism," Hayes denounced the neglect of this "community of heritage and outlook and interests in Europe and its whole American frontier." Of the "Atlantic community and the European civilization basic to it, we Americans," he wrote, "are co-heirs and co-developers, and probably in the future the leaders." After World War I America failed to prevent the disintegration of that community, and the world paid a terrible price. Now America must recognize that "the Atlantic community has been an outstanding fact and a prime factor of modern history" and must take its "rightful place in an international regional community of which the Atlantic is the inland sea."[7]

A major policy statement both political and academic by a leading scholar/diplomat, Hayes's famous speech formed a bridge between public policy commentary and historical scholarship. But he and Hoffman, though perhaps more zealous than others, were not alone in responding historically to the Atlanticist atmosphere of the time. Frederick Tolles, recalling in 1960 the origins of the thinking behind his *Quakers and the Atlantic Culture,* was explicit in noting the connection:

> We first became familiar with the idea of the Atlantic Community as a strategic concept during the Second World War, but the Atlantic Community as a cultural fact was a matter of almost everyday experience to English-speaking people in the seventeenth and eighteenth centuries. Historians . . . have only recently begun to treat the Atlantic civilization as a single unit.

"I don't know," he wrote, "whether the term 'Atlantic culture', which I have used in my title, is yet an expression in common use or not. But if it is not, it should be. For it seems to me as useful and necessary a term as the indispensable phrase 'Mediterranean culture', which we use to denominate the civilization of the ancient world."[8]

In fact the term "Atlantic," with implications that the word had not had before, was by then beginning to be commonly used by historians. It was appearing here and there in a scattering of unrelated probes in history, especially of the history of the preindustrial period, and wherever it appeared it expressed a growing sense, reflective of the Atlanticist climate of opinion, that the Atlantic world was a unit, historically as well as politically. The term as now used suggested conceptual breadth and elevation that gave a heightened meaning to otherwise local, prosaic historical material.

Thus in 1946 an English historian, H. Hale Bellot, in an address entitled "Atlantic History," urged the schoolteachers of history in Britain to include American history in their curricula not as

> a separate national story to be laid arbitrarily alongside the national history of Great Britain, but [as] an integral and vital part of the history of those areas, European and American alike, which border upon the North Atlantic, and something without an understanding of which the history of western Europe in the nineteenth and twentieth centuries is incomprehensible.

For, he explained, the great historical developments in the United States—economic, political, and demographic— "are not American but Atlantic phenomena. The boundary between the area which is settled and that which supplied the settlers and the capital resources is not the Atlantic seaboard, the political boundary of the United States, but the Appalachian range, the watershed of the Atlantic basin."[9]

The next year, 1947, Jacques Godechot, professor of history at the University of Toulouse and a well-known historian of the French Revolution, made his first, unsure foray into a subject that would occupy him for the rest of his life. In his *Histoire de l'Atlantique,* written when he was teaching at the French naval academy, he set out, in a luminous introduction, a view of the Atlantic as an "immense plain without landmarks, a gigantic 'no man's land,' an ageless desert"—yet an area with a history, "a long and weighty history" marked by great flows of wealth in times of peace and great battles in times of war. And like land areas, it had been transformed by modern technology. "To write the history of the Atlantic is not, therefore, an absurdity," for that history illuminates the history of everything to the east of it, and particularly the history of modern France. Godechot continued the themes of his introduction at the end of the book in a concluding paragraph entitled "toward an Atlantic civilization," but despite its imaginative framework, in its substance the volume was a narrow account of maritime history, chiefly French naval history, from 600 BC to 1946. Since the monographic foundations for such an immense survey were lacking, C. N. Parkinson wrote in one of the few reviews the book received, the effort, he decided, was "premature." And furthermore, he noted, Godechot was ignorant of many of the works that did exist, and "his conclusions are often wrong."[10]

But though Godechot's energy may have been "misapplied" (Parkinson), he had identified in this early effort and embraced, however briefly, tentatively, and rhetorically, a theme that others were independently beginning to touch on in different ways, in different places, for different reasons, and from different angles of vision. The coincidences were at times remarkable. In 1948 the Belgian royalist Jacques Pirenne published in Neuchâtel, Switzerland, the third volume of his *Grands Courants de l'Histoire Universelle,* which contains a section entitled "The Atlantic Ocean Forms an Interior Sea around which Western Civilization Develops." A few months later, the same idea was elaborated in a book published by Michael Kraus, of the City University of New York, entitled *Atlantic Civilization: Eighteenth-Century Origins,* in which he described the impact of eighteenth-century North America on Europe, arguing, largely on the basis of literary documents, that North America accelerated the growth of Europe's economy, helped make European class relations more fluid, and stimulated the imagination of Europe's poets, philosophers, artists, and scientists. The resulting construction of an Atlantic civilization, he concluded—a joint enterprise of the New World and the Old—"is one of the most remarkable developments in world history."

The next year, 1950, saw a flurry of statements suggesting other dimensions. From Portugal came a paper by V. M. Godinho, anticipating his later general work on the economy of the Portuguese empire, under the general title of "problems in Atlantic economy," though in fact it concentrated on the Portuguese-Brazilian sugar trade. Simultaneously, Max Silberschmidt, of the University of Zurich, presented a paper to the International Congress of Historical Sciences subtitled "Die Atlantische Gemeinschaft" in which he urged historians to recognize the fact that the dominance of the separate European nations in the nineteenth century, each pursuing its own fortunes, had given way, through two world wars, to the overwhelming power of America, which had led to the integration of Europe into a pan-Atlantic community. Three years later (1953) Pierre and Huguette Chaunu published in their essay "Économie atlantique. Économie mondiale" the prospectus of their vast statistical study, *Séville et l'Atlantique,* which would appear in eleven volumes between 1955 and 1959. Though "Atlantique" was for them a familiar and convenient term to describe a phenomenon that was not different in kind from what Haring had dealt with in his *Trade and Navigation between Spain and the Indies* (1918), their language was more elevated, more suggestive of a different plane of thought. Lucien Febvre, in his preface to the first of the Chaunus' volumes, caught the implications, construing the subject as *"l'espace atlantique,"* a phrase which Pierre Chaunu would incorporate into a characteristic *Annales* formulation, *"les 'structures' et les 'conjonctures' de l'espace Atlantique."*[11]

But by then, as this Atlanticist awareness grew, other historians, moving in from different intellectual origins, were making the first approaches to a general conceptualization. Almost simultaneously (1953–54) from Ghent in Belgium, from Toulouse in France, from Princeton in the United States, and from UNESCO headquarters in Paris came statements that addressed the subject directly. The first formulation came in an essay by the Belgian medievalist and economic historian, Charles Verlinden, published in the first volume (1953) of the trilingual *Journal of World History*. Long a student of slavery in medieval Europe and of transoceanic commerce, Verlinden declared, in a paper entitled "Les Origines coloniales de la civilisation atlantique," that

> it is certain that an Atlantic civilization exists today and that the nations of western Europe as well as of the two Americas and South Africa are daily becoming more completely integrated within it. A civilization nourished by and based on ideas, institutions, and forms of organization and work of common origins has developed gradually on the two coasts of the new Mediterranean of our time: the Atlantic Ocean.
>
> For the specialist in intellectual history the origins of that common civilization is to be found in the eighteenth century. But the development of cultural relations in a larger sense would have been impossible in the Atlantic world without the existence of institutional, economic, social, and administrative foundations and precedents created in western Europe during preceding centuries, that is, the middle ages. More than that, a continuity exists between certain colonial developments in the Mediterranean world in the late middle ages and the great colonizing enterprises in the Atlantic region in the sixteenth and seventeenth centuries.

Verlinden thereupon proceeded to sketch the lines of continuity that had led to the origins of "Atlantic civilization." [12]

Verlinden's "Les Origines coloniales" was a true "essay"—a probe, a test, a conjectural point of view and a new perspective—which, he believed, had various possibilities for both scholarship and public policy and suggested challenging historical questions. Was "Atlantic civilization" not unique, he asked, in its integral bindings between common economic and institutional structures and cultural life, as opposed to the Islamic and Buddhist worlds, which would appear to be unified only by a common religion overlaid on very different socioeconomic infrastructures? Was Atlantic civilization not distinctive in its formation around an interior ocean? Had not colonization via maritime routes, as opposed to overland linkages, made possible a distinctive political world? These were questions, Verlinden said, that one could well imagine an international symposium under UNESCO auspices discussing, with results that might help future statesmen avoid blunders.

Reference to UNESCO must have come easily to Verlinden since he was already involved in a project under that body's auspices that was relevant to his emerging interests. In 1953 he drafted for that organization a program for the "Study of the Cultural Relations between the Old World and the New." Two international conferences of "writers, philosophers, artists, educators, historians, sociologists, etc., from various countries of Europe and the Americas" were to be held in São Paulo and Geneva, to "suggest the best ways of strengthening intellectual and moral ties between the old and new worlds." Years before,

he noted, the League of Nations had sponsored a conference on the relationship between Europe and Latin America. But the questions raised then had not been "ripe for
fruitful discussion. Fortunately, men of the Old and New
Worlds are today much more conscious of their mutual
interests and interrelations and better prepared to understand them objectively." The two conferences duly met,
and the result was a volume, *Le Nouveau Monde et
l'Europe* (Neuchâtel, 1955), with contributions in writing or recorded discussion by such luminaries as Lucien
Febvre, George Boas, Andre Maurois, Max Silberschmidt,
Richard McKeon, Czeslaw Milosz, Jean Wahl, Alexandre
Koyré, Georges Bataille, Magnus Mörner, and a group of
notable Latin American scholars.[13]

Verlinden himself did not participate directly in these
conferences, but he was a key player in another multinational historical project of the early 1950s that had a pe-
culiar relevance to Atlantic history. In 1947, at the sugges-
tion of the University of Pennsylvania's Latin Americanist
Arthur Whitaker, the Commission on History of the Pan-
american Institute of Geography and History engaged an
international phalanx of historians, including Verlinden,
led by the Mexican historian Silvio Zavala to produce a
multivolume series of monographs on the history of the
Western Hemisphere and three synthetic volumes covering the entire subject. Inspired in part by Herbert Bolton's
famous argument in his "Epic of Greater America" that
the Americas must be understood in terms of their common history, and responding to pan-American political

interests, the Commission's "Program of the History of America" extended through the entire decade of the 1950s and produced in 1962 the designated detailed monographs and the three synthetic volumes: on the pre-colonial period, by Pedro Armillas (Mexico); on the colonial period, by Zavala (Mexico); and on the national period, by Charles Griffin (United States). The project was recognized by Roy Nichols, professor of history at the University of Pennsylvania, among others, as a heroic effort in grand-scale history, a feat of "comprehensive planning and . . . a tremendous concentration of skill and effort." Zavala's two-volume synthesis of the colonial period alone was seen as "the fruit of tremendous industry . . . magnificent bibliographical coverage and a high degree of sophisticated insight and understanding."[14]

There had been great hopes that this complex historical work would reach into all levels of Americans' awareness and become a permanent part of history instruction in the two continents' schools and universities. But the underlying concept had come under criticism, partly because the differences between North and South—between Latin America and Anglo-America—were more apparent than the similarities or parallels, partly because of the breadth of coauthorship and "the absence of any clear agreement on the topics and methods of the future," but mainly because the separation of the Western Hemisphere from Europe was unrealistic. "Interaction between America and Europe," John Parry wrote in a respectful but pointed critique, "was more continuous and more significant than in-

teraction between one American country and another . . .
Many colonies—perhaps most—lived their own lives, and
their own histories, without being very much affected
by the fortunes of their neighbors." For Verlinden even
more emphatically, the European connections were cru-
cial. Latin America, he wrote in 1966, was "a kind of extension of Europe which acquired a culture and features
whose European basis was readily apparent . . . The massive contribution made by the European population to
America has made of this double continent a new Europe
. . . [a] specifically Atlantic human composition" to which
Africa "is fatally linked." And in his narrative textbook of
the same year, *Les Origines de la Civilisation Atlantique,*
he set out to consider the "Atlantic zone and its significance in the evolution of the world," stressing the recipro-
cal relationships of "Atlantic Europe, the two Americas,
and Africa" and the formation of a single great cultural
area by the acculturation of the indigenous populations
and the progressive adaptation of colonial societies to new
natural and human environments.

Zavala struggled to resolve the issue, proposing a "dual
focus" and insisting on "a flexibility of judgment in order
to realize the complexity of the phenomena." But the
problem went beyond "the unity or diversity in the history of the New World" into the deeper issue of pan-
Atlantic relations. By 1964, when Lewis Hanke edited a
collection of essays on Bolton's thesis and the History
of America project, the conclusion was that the great effort in pan-American history had had "relatively little im-

pact"; the product, Charles Gibson wrote, was "far from the clarion call that the supporters of the program . . . exuberantly predicted." The project had failed to reshape Americans' historical awareness.[15]

It was in the midst of this hemispheric effort and two years after Verlinden's first essay on the colonial origins of Atlantic civilization had appeared that the first direct attempt at a comprehensive conceptualization of the idea of Atlantic history was published. It was a striking collaborative effort by two historians for whom that idea was compelling.

In 1954–55 Godechot was a visiting research fellow at Princeton University. During those months he collaborated with his host, Robert Palmer, who remembered Godechot's *Histoire de l'Atlantique* and who had just published two articles on the eighteenth-century revolutionary movement as a phenomenon "more or less common to an Atlantic civilization." Revolutionary aims and sympathies, Palmer had written, "existed throughout Europe and America . . . They were not imitated from the French." A general revolutionary agitation had arisen everywhere in the Western world "out of local, genuine and specific causes." With these ideas and those of Godechot's earlier *Histoire de l'Atlantique* in mind, the two men prepared a joint paper, entitled "Le Problème de l'Atlantique," for presentation to the Tenth International History Congress in Rome.[16]

After due acknowledgment of the politics of the Atlantic Charter and of the journalists and historians who had broached the subject, the authors swept broadly, in sixty-two pages, over all the issues, historical and contemporary, that they could associate with the concept of Atlantic civilization. A diffuse, learned inquiry, it looped back on itself to pose challenging questions. Had not the Atlantic Ocean, like Braudel's Mediterranean, "become a basin around which a new civilization slowly formed, an *Atlantic* civilization? . . . Barrier or bond, such is the problem of the Atlantic." Had there been *one* Atlantic civilization in the past, and if it still exists has it diverged into several? Was not Arthur Whitaker right in thinking that Latin America and English America formed two sides of an "Atlantic triangle" of which Europe formed the third—and that only during the Enlightenment had there been "a certain uniformity in ideas and values"? And further, since the Atlantic world had been created by Europe's influence on the Western Hemisphere, did not the enfeeblement of Europe after two world wars mark the end of "the first great period of American history," which had begun in 1492?

Godechot and Palmer's answers came in eight sections, which followed a discussion of Braudel's apparently inspirational notion that the history of an ocean involves the history of the lands that surround it. Thus launched, the authors moved on to a discussion of the "permeability" of transoceanic routes and communications, England's dominance of the Atlantic waters, the North Atlantic triangle of Canada, Britain, and the United States, and the history of commerce in the Atlantic basin. They then circled back to the question of whether there has been *one* Atlantic civilization or several. One, surely, they wrote, if one contrasts Orient and Occident. For it was clear that the civilization of the Atlantic world, for all its internal differences, having preserved in its foundations the *"idées maîtresses"* of Judeo-Christianity, Roman law, and Greek reason,

> has been able to create a society more liberal and more dynamic than that of the East of the old continent. To an ever growing extent it attached the highest value to liberty and the perfectibility of the individual, to the idea of law as an expression of justice, to the conception of a legitimate power as defined and limited by law. It is less and less disposed to follow custom passively and to submit to force.

Yet, the authors wrote, Atlantic civilization has never been static or monolithic, and they proceeded to survey the recent historical writing that had probed, one way and another, the multitudinous problems of and variations within Atlantic history as it had developed since the eighteenth century. Their conclusion, after a detour into the vagueness of the term "civilization" as defined by anthropologists, was that America and Europe had been closely united in the era of the eighteenth-century revolutions, but since then, despite their common culture, they had grown apart.

> If the asymmetry between the United States and Europe in the sphere of economics could be reduced, if the poverty of Latin America could be diminished, if Europe continues

to grow stronger, if the USSR continues to live apart, if the great Asiatic civilizations develop their nationalisms and their hostile dispositions to the West, then there will be a renewal in the future and a development not only of an Atlantic diplomatic alliance but also of a western or Atlantic civilization.[17]

In part still political and ideological, though mainly didactic and academic, and suffused with an air of discovery, Godechot and Palmer's essay met with what Palmer later called "a surprisingly cool reception" at the International History Congress. In fact the reception was clangorous, at times acerb. A Harvard professor declared that the idea of Atlantic history had been his in the first place, and then criticized the authors for failing to anticipate the permeability of air space. One British historian said he resented being "rounded-up and challenged to raise his sights and put on philosopher's spectacles"; another declared that the idea of an Atlantic Community, while "of overwhelming importance today," was a temporary response to Soviet policy and would change; and a third declared that "the concept of the Atlantic Community [was but] a step towards one world." A Polish delegate rejected any significant differences between Western and Eastern Europe, pointing out that a bust of Washington had been erected in the royal palace in Warsaw and that Poles had fought in the American Revolution and had had the most active *(plus vifs)* associations with the French Revolution. And then a Marxist historian, after ridiculing the authors' definition of Western civilization as vague and arbitrary (one might as well define it as the world "within which witches were systematically persecuted and burned . . . (Laughter)," declared that the paper obscured the fundamental economic and social developments of the past few centuries, and denied that America and Western Europe had developed toward freedom while the East had not.

Godechot replied at length, insisting that he and Palmer had not flatly affirmed the existence of an Atlantic civilization but had only posed the question of its existence, a question that only time would answer, and concluded that the passionate responses the paper had evoked proved that posing the question had been useful.[18]

Palmer was less complacent, and less forgiving. Thirty-five years later he recalled of the responses that "a famous British diplomatic historian said that there was no such subject. A then young but later famous British Marxist historian said that he hoped that no such subject would ever be heard of at any future congress. We were accused, then and later, of being apologists for NATO and the newfangled idea of an Atlantic community." And the reception continued to be cool when the two authors' major works appeared, to which the essay of 1955 had been a prologue. Godechot's two-volume *La Grande Nation*, published in 1956, traced the spread of the French Revolution and its ideas throughout Europe, and incidentally in America (a subject Godechot would expand in a later book, *France and the Atlantic Revolution of the Eigh-*

teenth Century, 1965). Palmer's even more ambitious *The Age of the Democratic Revolution* (two volumes, 1959, 1964) drew the American Revolution directly into the larger picture and assigned it a key creative role in the whole Atlantic phenomenon. These were imaginative, notable, large-scale works, but, Palmer said, "the reception continued to be mainly negative."

> Not only Marxism but a certain French national self-image was offended. We were thought to downgrade the importance or uniqueness of the French Revolution by diluting it into a vague general international disturbance. Godechot and I were thereafter paired as two proponents, or indeed the only proponents, of something called the Atlantic Revolution, a phrase that he used more often than I did.[19]

Palmer continued to reply to critics of the Atlantic Revolution thesis. But though his view of the French Revolution was bypassed by, or absorbed in, that of Albert Soboul and other historians of the Revolution, his and Godechot's tentative, ruminating sketch of the Atlantic world as a community, especially in the late eighteenth century, gradually acquired substance and certitude. For their view, however inconclusive and unsure and however uncomfortably close to the great politico-ideological concerns of the postwar years, had developed not abstractly or deductively but empirically, from their own documentary research. Their publications marked the point at which the external, public orientation of historians' thought merged with the internal propulsions of scholarship, the inner logic of historical inquiry.

II

For scholarship has its own internal dynamics. The inductive elaboration of research in specific subjects that has no other purpose than its own fulfillment—research that is in no way an epiphenomenon reflecting something more determinative than itself—is an independent creative force. However reflective of its environment and responsive to social pressures and rewards, it has its own logic, its own natural sequences, often dialectical; it has its own evolutionary process impelled forward by the sudden punctuations of seminal discoveries and interpretations. In these years the interior impulses and logic of scholarship were leading in directions congruent with and supportive of the postwar political perspectives that had brought into focus the idea of an Atlantic community. This was part of a more general development. In several areas the constant enrichment of historical research, the propulsions of inquiry during years of immense expansion in the academic world and an unprecedented amount of international communication and interaction among scholars, led to a rescaling of perspective in which the basic dimensions of discussion were larger than the traditional units within which the research had begun. Simply by the force of scholarship itself, what I have elsewhere called large-scale spatial orbits developing through time were becoming visible as they had not been before, and within them patterns of filiation and derivation.[20] One major locus for such expanding research lay in the area of Atlantic history.

Before the decade of the 1950s had passed, Pierre Chaunu, embarking alone on a four-volume interpretation of the seven volumes of data (3,880 pages) he and Huguette Chaunu had published in their *Séville et l'Atlantique,* was moved to contemplate not simply Seville's Atlantic commerce in all its aspects but "the history of an ocean." Analyzing his mountains of documents and statistics, he wrote that the Atlantic was the first ocean—as opposed to Braudel's inland sea—"to have been regularly crossed, the first to find itself at the heart of an economy, indeed of a civilization, diverse, complex, multiple . . . yet essentially one." He organized his four-volume interpretation of Ibero-Atlantic civilization in terms of the French *Annalistes' "structures et conjonctures,"* presenting in the first two volumes the constituent elements and in the final two volumes the movement of things—the modifications, variables, gradients, and speed. The result was a prodigious panorama—not only the history of a trading area during the hegemony of Spain, not only the history of two continents in their interaction together with the involvements of their "archipelagos" (outlying islands, east and west) but of the entire Ibero-American world. To be sure, one critic wrote, the work was verbose, long-winded, and repetitious—at times its outline was lost in the sheer immensity of detail—but its general effect was simply "overwhelming" *(aplastante).* Haring had covered some of the same ground, but not with Chaunu's "breadth of vision, scope of scholarship, and maturity of thinking." Chaunu had elevated the subject to "an infinitely higher level," and "in such a way as to make possible a fresh and immensely rewarding look at reality."[21]

While Chaunu was completing his titanic *oeuvre,* other important lines of historical scholarship were developing in the three decades after World War II which added substantial detail to the historical concept of a coherent Atlantic world. Developments in demographic history, originating in France in the 1950s, then spreading to England, the United States, and elsewhere, spilled over naturally into migration studies that added a new, profound dimension to Atlantic studies.

Thus the Atlantic slave trade had long been a matter of great historical interest, but it took on new importance with the publication, in 1969, of Philip Curtin's *The Atlantic Slave Trade: A Census.* That seminal study of the printed tabulations of the Hispanic, English, and French slave trades had emerged from Curtin's earlier book on nineteenth-century Jamaica (1955), originally a dissertation of 1953. There Curtin, a student of British history, had discovered not only what he called a South Atlantic System—"a regional economic, political, and social order of which Jamaica had been a part"—but two distinct though intertwined cultures and economies on the island—African and European—whose tensions led to sudden disruptions and ultimately decline. Thereafter his inquiries had deepened and broadened to include questions of the African sources of Jamaican culture, the geographical origins of the island's slave population, and their numbers and condition. And they had led him as much to the data and ideas of African anthropologists as to those of British historians—and had led also to questions of epidemiology and statistics, all of which went into the writing of the seminal slave-trade census book. After that the links to even broader, more expansive studies of the African diaspora multiplied: notably, his *Image of Africa,* a collection of slave narratives, a study of epidemics, and a monograph on Senegambia. All of this inspired a generation of increasingly sophisticated studies of the slave trade and of slavery and the rise of "the Atlantic system."[22] The growing library of writings on the slave trade would culminate in 1999 in the publication of the computerized *Trans-Atlantic Slave Trade* database, a collaborative product of four historians (English, Canadian, and American) which assembled in systematic, computer-searchable form a vast array of information related to some 27,000 slave voyages, two-thirds of the estimated total—Spanish, Portuguese, Dutch, British, and North American. The links between Curtin's early *Jamaicas* and the massive database forty-four years later that contained in itself a vast human panorama of Atlantic history, a tragic network linking Africa, Europe, and the Americas, had grown naturally, organically, in response to the creative impulses of scholarship, as the subject's importance, enhanced but not defined by social pressures, had become clear.[23]

In the same years the demographic history of the Atlantic world expanded in other directions. In North America, it took the form of migration studies of distinctive ethnic groups and the social structure of immigrant settlements. In Hispanic America the concentration was primarily on the original size, radical decline, and nature of the indigenous populations, on the transatlantic migration of Europeans, and on the complex social world that resulted from the encounters of the two worlds, both interacting with the forced migrants from Africa. In both North and South knowledge expanded logically, enlarged by the sudden availability of computers, the adaptation of the innovative statistical techniques of historical demographers, and the ideas of social anthropologists.

In British America filiopiety, ethnic pride, and genealogical interests had long since spawned libraries of scattered, randomly collected data on transatlantic migrants, their origins, their families and group identities, their religious organizations and practices, and something of their customs and ways of life. All of that social miscellany could now be turned to systematic uses as a broad view of an emerging New World society became increasingly clear.

Accidentally preserved registries of transatlantic migrants from seventeenth- and eighteenth-century London and Bristol became vital sources. Questions that had been raised as early as 1934 could be answered more fully and the answers would initiate a stream of associated studies. The Bristol and London emigrant registries used by Abbot E. Smith in his 1947 study of the transatlantic migration of white servants and convicts, *Colonists in Bondage,* were reanalyzed more fully by Mildred Campbell in her "Social Origins of Some Early Americans" (1959) to sketch a distinctive picture of social recruitment. Her conclusions on the social level of the immigrants were disputed by a young economist, David Galenson (1978), defended by Campbell with new tabulations (1979), and finally in 1981 absorbed in the comprehensive statistical analysis of all the servant registries in Galenson's *White Servitude in Colonial America.* And there would be more beyond that. *Voyagers to the West* (1986) based an interpretation of all of Britain's emigrations to the Western Hemisphere on the eve of the Revolution on an exhaustive statistical analysis of the London registry that had first been used forty years earlier by Smith. And further still, Smith's early interest in convict emigration to America would be fulfilled in Roger Ekirch's definitive study of convict transportation, *Bound for America* (1987). The developments over four decades in this one corner of Atlantic historiography were continuous, led on from point to point by curiosity and the prospect of new, enhanced views.[24]

In other areas of North American history the same impulses proved to be equally creative—and nowhere more so than in the remarkable work of a generation of social historians of the seventeenth-century Chesapeake region. Beginning in the 1960s a group of young historians began burrowing in the voluminous archives of Maryland and Virginia and applied the techniques of the French demographers, refined by historians in England, to questions of social organization, family and household structure, and the labor force in the Upper South. The questions were fresh, the findings at times astonishing. Article followed article, with cross-references to the ongoing work; collaborations formed and reformed; archival data were assembled, published, analyzed and reanalyzed, until finally three successive collections of papers and a series of ancillary publications—all linked together and mutually reinforcing—revealed an Anglo-American plantation world that had never been known before: its unique, complex social structure, its deviations from metropolitan social models, and its web of connections with other parts of the Atlantic world. No extrinsic forces had been at work; the impulses that sustained this unusually creative enterprise were intrinsic: an interest in new questions, the availability of unused data and new techniques, and the excitement and satisfaction of recovering a lost world.[25]

The same possibilities were seen for the history of other groups within the British sphere. Understanding of the migration of German Protestants to eighteenth-century North America and their settlement there—long romanticized by ethnic pride—grew by similar efforts. The questions that arose, once the numbers were established and the European background examined, were intriguing. There were no obvious answers, and the attempt to find them led to ever more puzzling and interesting questions which spanned the Atlantic world and drew it together.

That half a million German Protestants fled from the

Palatinate, ruled in the later seventeenth century by reactionary Catholic princes, and from elsewhere in southwestern Germany, northern Switzerland, and southeastern France seeking refuge in more tolerant communities—that was no mystery. Nor were the decisions of the majority of that diaspora mysterious. They did the rational thing, and moved off a few hundred miles northeast to Protestant Prussia, which was trying to populate the Ostmark, or sailed down the Danube into Hapsburg lands where they were promised some degree of security. What *was* mysterious is why 100,000 of them did the irrational thing and undertook a grim trip down the Rhine where they had to pass through some forty tolls and barriers, to end up impoverished in Rotterdam, where they waited under difficult conditions, every passing day reducing their resources, until they could get passage to Southampton or Cowes. Once at those English transit points they again had long delays under even worse conditions, and then risked their lives on a three-thousand-mile ocean voyage in vessels little better than coastal schooners. Why did they do this, especially after the miseries of the enterprise became notorious in the villages of the Palatinate?[26]

Such questions were intriguing; they developed from earlier questions and answers, and they would lead to deeper studies of the cultural relations of the German communities and British North America.[27] Answers did not serve any greater purpose than to satisfy one's curiosity and resolve certain nagging anomalies; but once forthcoming, they led to a broadening understanding of the Atlantic world as a human community. So the existence of obscure German settlements in a remote corner of the present American state of Georgia in the early eighteenth century was shown to be an incidental consequence of the decision of the reactionary Archbishop of Salzburg to expel the evangelicals from that deeply provincial, mountainous mining region. The famous Archiepiscopacy of Salzburg, soon to be the scene of Mozart's triumphs and trials, and the obscure, primitive, frontier evangelical village of Ebenezer, Georgia, could be seen as part of the same story.[28]

Parallel efforts would be made to demonstrate the pan-Atlantic webs of association between other settler groups in British America and their original cultural hearths—in Ireland, Scotland, and the Netherlands. And beyond that would lie an effort to trace back into the regional subcultures of early modern Britain four deep-lying cultural strains in North American society—Puritan, Anglican, Quaker-Pietist, and north-border Scotch and Irish.[29]

In the same years, when the dimensions and inner complexity of the African-Atlantic diaspora were becoming clear and when the transoceanic history of immigration to and settlement in British America was being elaborated, Latin American historians too were finding in population history a key to an expansive view of their subject, far broader in scope than the traditional accounts of conquest and studies of imperial institutions. The initial problem, and for decades one of the most baffling, was the size of the indigenous population at the point of European contact and the magnitudes and causes of its catastrophic decline. It was a subject that had political overtones in that it was relevant to postwar concerns with the human costs of European imperialism and was relevant too to struggles over shades of racial differences in contemporary Latin American social and political life. But from the start the proliferating writing on Latin American population history was impelled by interests in and energized by controversies within the boundaries of historical scholarship.

The initial postwar impetus, a sweeping study of the indigenous population of all of the Americas by the Polish-born Venezuelan Angel Rosenblat, updating studies he had begun in Spain a decade earlier and superseding other estimates that went back to the 1920s, supported neither the "Black Legend" of Spanish-American history nor its reverse. Like the new social historians in Latin America in general, he had "stopped jousting directly with the Black Legend . . . [had] forsaken history rooted in moral outrage, either against Spanish atrocities and barbarities in the New World or against accounts which highlighted these excesses at the expense of Spanish contributions or achievements." His estimates (1945, revised 1954, 1967), based on loosely constructed back-projections, scattered contemporary estimates, and informed guesswork, were low, and touched off a spate of rejoinders and fresh statistical probes by a phalanx of "high estimators." The ensuing debate "expanded by leaps and bounds," a bitter critic of the "high estimators" later conceded, "incorporated new arguments and new forms of discourse . . . [and]

brought in concepts from a remarkably broad range of disciplines." The key players in this proliferation of technical research and writing (among them, besides Rosenblat: Lesley Simpson, Sherburne Cook, and Woodrow Borah at Berkeley, Magnus Mörner at Stockholm, Henry Dobyns at several American universities, and Richard Konetzke at Cologne) formed an international research community in the immediate postwar years whose mutual challenges, rivalries, and collaborations stimulated immense productivity. Cook and Borah's joint studies, largely of Mexican population history, fill three volumes (1971–1979). Mörner's bibliography from 1947 to 1980 includes 274 publications in five languages, with the focus on Latin American population history, a subject he would summarize in a masterful short survey, *Race Mixture in the History of Latin America* (1967). Mörner had no political agenda, however useful his findings might prove to be for those who did, and while the Berkeley group's and others' high estimates would later play into such heated cultural commentaries as David Stannard's *American Holocaust* and Kirkpatrick Sale's *The Conquest of Paradise,* their aim at the time was to contribute not to the culture wars but to a difficult technical inquiry—an inquiry which a generation later would still be unsettled. Their worst critic did not charge them with political correctness for their high initial estimates; the most he could say of their extra-historical motivation was that "a Zeitgeist" had affected them, which, "combined with a cadre and coterie spirit," inspired and impelled their work.[30]

But the demography of the indigenous population was not an isolated issue. It was closely bound in with the history of the conquering people and the immensely complex social world that resulted from their encounters with the natives. Developing in parallel with the migration studies of the British Atlantic were attempts to trace the movement of Iberians to Spanish and Portuguese America. In some cases the records were thin (especially for Brazil), in others difficult to access, but the Archive of the Indies' *Pasajeros a Indias,* roughly equivalent to the British emigration registries, made systematic study possible. The resulting analyses of the regional origins of the Spanish emigrants by Peter Boyd-Bowman, begun in 1952 with, he wrote, "no preconceived ideas" and summarized in 1973 and 1976, revealed a distinctive world in motion, part of the repeopling of the Western Hemisphere. The statistically typical transatlantic voyager, he found largely on the basis of linguistic evidence, "was a poverty-stricken Andalusian male aged 27½, unmarried, unskilled and probably only semi-literate, driven by hunger to make his way to Peru in the employ of any man who would pay his passage and had secured the necessary permit." The typical woman was somewhat older, married, and accompanied by children and a servant or two; both were typically born and raised in Seville, "whose phonologically innovative dialect was already becoming standardized in all the ports of the Caribbean." Later it became clear that the Andalusian predominance would give way to a "broad cross-section of Castilians."[31] All of this was new to the history of Ibero-America—a new dimension of social history, a new sense of transoceanic linkages.

For Boyd-Bowman, language in its Atlantic context was a major concern, but it was relevant to other postwar historians opening up areas of Latin American social history that had scarcely been glimpsed before—"close readers" of a great variety of scattered sources who were able to use demographic information as it became available, but who went beyond it into the microreality of people's lives—to "fill in," James Lockhart wrote, "what it meant to be 'Spanish,' 'Indian,' and 'mestizo.'" Lockhart himself, one of the most masterful of the "close readers," had set out around 1960, he later wrote, simply to help expand knowledge of Latin American history and "make sense of the whole." He had thought much about scholars' motivations, including his own, and his conclusions were clear. Social historians like himself, he wrote in 1972,

> are more likely to be motivated by a positive fascination with their subject than by the moral outrage of the developmentalists . . . when there is a high degree of political or ideological interest in a subject, its study may veer far indeed from that steady march through the sources which, though perhaps blind, is natural, organic, and in a sense logical.

It was to discover what Lockhart called the "core" of Ibero-American society—for its own sake—that the social historians of the 1960s and 1970s undertook "the close study of a certain segment of social reality" beyond the concerns of their academic predecessors and deeper and more systematic than what Lockhart called Gilberto Freyre's "impressionistic levity" shaped by "twentieth-century political-institutional movements." Their search was not for the precontact autochthonous world, which was the realm of anthropologists and archaeologists, but for the human reality of Ibero-America, which was the creation of the encounters of the people of three conti-nents. The reality they found was multilayered—complex blendings of behavior patterns, lifestyles, and social struc-tures, the more fine-grained the analysis the more com-plex the picture. So the inner reality of the haciendas and encomiendas proved not to be what it had seemed to be, nor were the families and households of either natives or Spanish or mestizos. Study of local court trials began to reveal "the inner structure of a whole social milieu." Official life turned out to be intertwined in unexpected ways with social life, and the Luso-Brazilian world seen through the important lay brotherhoods appeared to be "a complete European-type urban-oriented society in opera-tion." Group biographies—prosopography—of audiencia judges, of merchants, of local officials, and of the people on the great estates revealed social structures that had not been seen before, as did Lockhart's study of the obscure people who accompanied the famous conquerors, *The Men of Cajamarca,* and David Brading's *Miners and Mer-chants* in Guanajuato. So too new views of the inner lives of the *castas* could be glimpsed and, in a critical develop-ment of the period, a realistic picture of the increasingly powerful creole aristocracy could be sketched—their ethnic composition, cultural attainments, and politics.

What propelled this rapid proliferation of Latin American social history was what Lockhart called "the inner logic of the subject"[32]—and that logic brought together elements that naturally combined into a pan-Atlantic mosaic, the grout lines of which were provided by the economic historians.

Earlier historians—Chaunu, Mauro, Godinho, Haring, Hamilton, Vicens Vives—had produced the elements for the construction of an Atlantic economic system bound together by a multitude of trading networks, monetary and capital flows, intercontinental labor markets, and pan-oceanic distribution patterns. Most of these studies had been confined, however, to national boundaries, partly because the sources were concentrated in national archives, partly because the doctrines of mercantilism were assumed to have been effective in practice, and partly because historians were used to thinking in nationalist categories. The younger postwar economic historians pressed against these limitations and began to uncover signs of a more complex world.

By the late 1960s Stanley and Barbara Stein, who would become leading economic historians of colonial Latin America, could already see the outline of a system that, because of Spain's failure to develop its own industrial base, drew into the commerce of Spanish America all of the major goods suppliers of Western Europe. By 1700 Andalusian monopolists of Spanish-American trade, the

Steins reported, were in fact "mere fronts for Genoese, French, Dutch, and English resident and non-resident merchants," and the Methuen Treaty of 1703 drew Portugal and Brazil "into a web of economic imperialism whose center was England." The entire Ibero-American commercial system, it had become clear, had been penetrated by foreign interests; and it was increasingly evident, from the research of the 1950s and 1960s, that the formal state-structured commercial system was a mere façade over the reality of a multinational dominance of Spain's economy.

Elsewhere, in these years, economic historians developed the sense that any vital part of the Atlantic economy could only be understood in terms of the whole, and that formal prescriptions did not describe reality. The great American mining industry, with its complexes of mobilized labor, ore sources, furnaces, mills, and refineries, was now seen, in new works by P. J. Bakewell and David Brading, in a broad Atlantic perspective that included details on mercury production in Spain, banking maneuvers in Germany, taxation policies and regulation in Madrid, and, in greater detail than before, the impact of bullion production on Spain's economy and foreign relations and on Europe's trading system as well. The attendant price rise came first to Spain, G. N. Clark wrote, "then it spread through all the countries west of Russia and the Turkish empire, more rapidly in some and less rapidly in others as they were able to get their share of American treasure by exchanging goods for silver . . . the old world of landlords and peasants found it harder to carry on; the traders and bankers found it easier, and capitalism advanced." Potosí, Lewis Hanke wrote in an early postwar survey of the history of that great mining center, had "a sort of wild-west atmosphere," crowded not only with Spaniards and *castas* of all kinds but with such a variety of foreigners that the Crown became alarmed.[33]

So too in other spheres there was a broadening vision of economic life. Jacob Price, like Curtin originally a British historian, found in his dissertation of 1954 on the British Treasury and the tobacco trade, presumably restricted to British marketing, a subject that would come to involve not only Britain and North America but much of the commercial economy of Western Europe and its colonies. His essays, which would be collected in three volumes, spread out logically from the tobacco trade to Scottish merchandizing, credit mechanisms, Quaker business families, and the manipulations of trade balances. His "Tobacco Adventure to Russia" (1961) traced the efforts of a syndicate of English and Russian merchants and diplomats under Peter the Great to monopolize the entire Russian market for tobacco. The great project failed at the last moment because of incompetence and greed, but one cannot help speculating what the consequences would have been if, as was likely, it had succeeded. If tobacco production in America had risen to satisfy the potential Russian market there would have been a huge expansion of cultivation; great pressure on the labor supply, which would have intensified the slave trade and other population movements; and soaring profits for American planters and English middlemen. The fates of merchants, farmers, servants, and slaves in the tobacco-producing lands of the Western Hemisphere would thereafter have been intimately tied to the habits of tobacco smokers in Russian cities, towns, and country estates. But even without the Russian tobacco contract, Europe and America were drawn together in this line of trade as in others. Price's two-volume magnum opus *France and the Chesapeake* (1973) brought together in great detail aspects of finance, commerce, society, and statecraft in France, Britain, and the Chesapeake region.[34]

The "Atlantic" dimension of the early modern economic history of the Western world seemed to illuminate the most local, provincial developments, whether in La Rochelle, on the eastern shore of Chesapeake Bay, in Bristol, England, in a variety of West Indian and Latin American port towns, or in New England. Early in this new phase of historical writing it became clear that the merchants of seventeenth-century New England were dependent for their profits not on a stable triangular trade but on an unstable, flexible, multilateral geometry of trade that shifted in such unpredictable ways, depending on the vagaries of local gluts and dearths, that success required marketing agents of extreme reliability and skill, capable of clever extemporization and shrewd risk-taking. As a consequence New England's earliest trading network throughout the Atlantic basin became a kinship network, as merchant families sent out the people they could best trust—sons and loyal in-laws—to man the families' trade in England, Ireland, the Wine Islands, the Caribbean, and the southern mainland colonies. And what family ties did for the New England families, religious affiliations did for Pennsylvania's Quaker merchants. Their coreligionists spread out through the Atlantic ports to manage the trade from and to Philadelphia. Young sons of trading families everywhere—in England as in Spain, in the Netherlands as in France—were sent abroad to learn the business at various locations throughout the Atlantic basin, to meet the people they would later have to deal with, and to pick up what they could of the most modern techniques of commerce.[35]

The emphasis on the human, individual, entrepreneurial aspects of commerce cast new light on old problems in the linkages within the Atlantic system. By examining not the formal structure of the Dutch West India Company but the people who devised that institution and controlled it, one could see that the failure of the company, which had tentacles throughout the Caribbean and reached into North and South America, did not mean the failure of the major players in the company. They knew how to exploit the company, how to circumvent its problems and continue to profit as individual traders in the company's once-monopolized territory, and how to reach beyond its scope into new enterprises on the Caribbean islands and the South American mainland.[36]

The centripetal forces at work in the Atlantic world of the seventeenth and eighteenth centuries were not, however, restricted to demography, the labor markets, and the economy. One of the major developments in the historiography of the postwar generation—impelled by the inner forces of scholarship, by the curiosity aroused by newly gathered information and new questions generated dialectically by answers to old questions—was a deeper understanding of the mechanisms of Atlantic politics.

Politics, that is, not government. The formal institutional structures of government in the Spanish, Portuguese, and British empires of that era had long been known. But for reasons that lay deep in historical thinking in the 1960s and 1970s one felt the necessity to go beyond institutions to the people who controlled these structures, who exploited them and made them work—beyond the structure of power, in other words, to the uses of power, the users of power, and the competition of individuals and factions for the benefits of power. And when that subject—politics—emerged with its own structure, there was revealed a mass of intricate connections throughout the Atlantic world which had not been seen before.[37]

Spain's empire—profoundly different from Britain's and France's in the depth and complexity of its governance and its constitutional relation to the metropolis—was not unique in the pan-Atlantic nature of its politics. It was governed by echelons of Crown officials who formed a network of bureaucrats spread out across the empire's great spaces. The supreme executives were the viceroys, governors, and presidents—92 viceroys were appointed before 1808. Beneath them were the regional audiencia judges—697 were appointed after 1687; 70–100 were in place at any given time. The audiencia judges served in lifetime positions as jurists, local magistrates, administrators, and subcontracting advisors and managers for corporate interests. And beneath them were ranges of lesser officials down to the local levels. All of the main appointees—viceroys and audiencia judges—gained their positions through the intricacies of court politics and were expected to serve as political surrogates. There were necessary qualifications: for the audiencia judges noble background, economic substance, and university training in law. But the sufficient conditions were political solicitation at court, persistent currying of favors, and cultivation of influential connections—a process of political maneuvering that could take years or even decades before an appointment was achieved. And thereafter one had to keep afloat politically not only in the turmoils of factional disputes in America but also in the intrigues at court. Many audiencia judges—even those who had bought their offices in the period of the Crown's destitution—felt it necessary to keep personal agents in Madrid to protect their interests, a practice that was formalized in the 1770s. Such political backstopping was particularly necessary for the American-born judges (39 percent of those whose background is known), whose Spanish contacts were insecure.

Imperial governance was no less political in Brazil, though on a smaller scale, and in the British case the politics of governance, also uncovered in writings of the 1960s and 1970s, was simply blatant. Office holding in the British Atlantic colonies was a direct part of the patronage system at the heart of eighteenth-century British politics.

The offices available in the colonies—from the most lucrative, like the major governorships, to the most petty, like tidewaiters in the minor ports—were within the gift of the patronage bosses in England and were distributed within the pressures of the system they managed. The Duke of Newcastle in the mid-eighteenth century could dispose of 85 offices in the colonies—invaluable assets in political infighting; by the 1770s the number of places in the gift of his successors was 226, and they were bestowed as benefits with an eye, not to the needs and interests of the colonists or to the qualifications of the appointees but to the benefit of the factions in England these brokers served.[38] And a separate branch of political patronage linking Britain and the colonies involved the military. Nine-tenths of the royal provincial governors appointed between 1660 and 1727 were officers rewarded for military service. Nine of the field officers under the Duke of Marlborough in the battle of Blenheim in 1704 were rewarded with gifts of North American governorships.[39]

By the early 1970s it was clear that the Anglo-American political system was in its essence a huge network of "informal connections . . . mercantile, ecclesiastical, and ethnic interest groups that had corresponding 'branches' in London and the various colonies."[40] Creole leaders, like their counterparts in Latin America, competed openly for the benefits of government, supported royal authority only when it suited them, challenged it or ignored it when it was useful to do so, while working within institutions whose legitimacy was generally respected.

What happened at the political heart of the British,

Spanish, and Portuguese governments mattered to provincial politicians in America. Fortunes were made, power was gained and lost in America by the twists and turns of factional politics at home—even at times by the movement of power rivalries deep in continental Europe. Until 1768 the executive head of colonial affairs in Britain was the secretary of state for the southern department, whose jurisdiction extended to the whole of western Europe. The secretary's decisions with respect to the politics of the Western Hemisphere were shown to have been in part a function of involvements in Paris, Madrid, and Vienna.[41]

In many ways, then—in demographic, social, economic, and political history—the unit of discussion had broadened out to encompass the entire Atlantic basin. And the same can be said of intellectual history. There were signs by the early 1970s of an expanding scope of historical inquiry that would in some degree bring together elements of the mental worlds of Europe and America. Franco Venturi had begun his studies of the European sweep of Enlightenment ideas in the 1950s; by 1969, in his Trevelyan Lectures, he had extended his range and found the model for Europe's "new spirit of independence . . . in distant America." In the same years that Venturi was tracing the flow of ideas from Italy and France to the north and west Caroline Robbins was uncovering the vital tradition of reformist, republican, commonwealth thought that had coursed through opposition circles in Britain for a century after the seventeenth-century Revolution and that would find its fulfillment not in Britain itself but in the

North American colonies. And it was also in the 1950s that J. G. A. Pocock had begun his studies of English political ideologies, which would establish, first in a seminal article on Machiavelli, Harrington, and English political ideologies and ultimately in *The Machiavellian Moment,* the genealogy of what he called "the Atlantic republican tradition" from fifteenth-century Italy to early nineteenth-century America. By the late 1960s the process from Machiavelli through Harrington, Neville, and *Cato's Letters* to Madison and Jefferson seemed clear, and with it a sense of the pan-Atlantic unity of British-American political thought.[42]

The bindings were no less clear, though different in substance, in the Ibero-American world. There the initial problem was to determine whether Spain's colonies were, as they were said to be, mired in ignorance and obscurantism, blocked off from Europe's emerging Enlightenment by the grip of medieval scholasticism and a reactionary Church. Indications of a more favorable view had appeared before the war, but it was in the decade that followed that Irving Leonard was able to prove that "profane and fabulous" publications were circulating freely in Latin America. At the same time John T. Lanning, having tackled the problem of the level of academic culture in Spanish America, concluded that "instead of a cultural lag of three centuries behind Europe there was a hiatus in the Spanish colonies of approximately one generation from European innovator to American academician . . . Between 1780 and 1800, with fair allowance for transportation and isolation, the lag ceased to exist." Though no historian claimed that the intellectual world in Latin America was entirely liberal and free, and though it was not yet clear how far Newtonian and Cartesian doctrines were incorporated into colonial thought, by the early 1950s it was evident that at least the most sophisticated circles in Spain's Atlantic empire shared in the advanced culture of Enlightenment Europe.[43]

THE HISTORIANS' WORLD, no less than the public world, had been transformed in the two or three decades that followed World War II. That among the changes was a convergence in identifying the Atlantic region as a distinctive stage of action was not the result of design or manipulation. The historians who wrote on topics that touched on Atlantic history came to it from many angles, for many reasons, from many motives. Some were simply pursuing narrow, parochial interests that proved to have wider boundaries than they had expected; some were determined to explore the wider reaches of established inquiries; most were following the logic of the subject as it unfolded. None were projecting contemporary politics back into history, but few were unaware of the struggle around them to identify and protect what Lippmann had called "the profound web of interest which joins together the western world." As historians, they were disengaged from politics, but they were people of their time and their awareness found natural expression in the larger amplitudes of the field.

The shift in historical perspective was essentially spatial, and so it was a historical geographer who, at the end of this era, gave the fullest expression to what had happened in this short period of historical writing, and how the idea of Atlantic history had emerged. "We can see," D. W. Meinig wrote in 1986, that it was not simply "that the two great thrusts out of the two creative source regions carried two distinct versions of European civilization across the ocean, initiating a Catholic imperial America in the south and a Protestant commercial America in the north. But these direct extensions were increasingly caught up into larger Atlantic circuits binding together four continents, three races, and several cultural systems, complicating and blurring the processes of extension and transfer . . . The ocean had become the 'inland sea of Western Civilization,' a 'new Mediterranean' on a global scale, with old seats of culture on the east, a great frontier for expansion on the west, and a long and integral African shore." The Atlantic world was, Meinig writes,

> the scene of a vast interaction rather than merely the transfer of Europeans onto American shores. Instead of a European discovery of a new world, we might better consider it as a sudden and harsh encounter between two old worlds that transformed both and integrated them into a single New World. Our focus is upon the creation of new human geographies resulting from this interaction, and that means those developing not only westward upon the body of America but eastward upon the body of Europe, and inward upon and laterally along the body of Africa. For it is

certain that the geography of each was changed: radically on the American side . . . more subtly on the European side, with new movements of people, goods, capital, and information flowing through an established spatial system and slowly altering its proportions and directions; slowly and unevenly on the African side, making connections with existing commercial systems but eventually grotesquely altering the scale and meaning of old institutions.[44]

"*. . . a sudden and harsh encounter between two old worlds that transformed both and integrated them into a single New World*": this was the origin of Atlantic History.

II

On the Contours of
Atlantic History

"For the first time in human history," David Eltis has written of the early modern Atlantic world, there appeared a hemispheric "community"

> in the sense . . . that everyone living in it had values which if they were not shared around the Atlantic were certainly reshaped in some way by others living in different parts of the Atlantic basins, and . . . where events in one small geographical area were likely to stimulate a reaction—and not necessarily just economic—thousands of miles away. The result was, if not a single Atlantic society, a set of societies fundamentally different from what they would have been without participation in the new transatlantic network.[1]

Atlantic history—"a connecting element between European, North American, Caribbean, Latin American, and West African history," in the words of the leading German Atlanticist Horst Pietschmann—invites and has received methodological speculation of some subtlety: the possibilities of network analysis, the logic of comparative history, the applicability of the concept of "systems."[2] But history has its own elemental method, its basic principle of organization, which is narrative in the largest sense— chronological, developmental, transformative: the story of growth, change, and evanescence. And in this, Atlantic history is no exception. Large as the subject is in time and space, complex as it is in geographic, environmental, ethnographic, economic, and political terms, it too has basic phases of development and transformation; it too is comprehensible as a story in itself. Though no simple sketch can begin to encompass the story as a whole or even properly indicate its dimensions, the effort to suggest a possible outline of the whole, or of certain aspects of the whole, may at least help clarify some basic themes.

Any attempt to do this must overcome two limitations inherited from the received historiography: first, the assumption that Atlantic history is the combination of several national histories and their extensions overseas—that its essential character lies in the aggregation of four or five discrete European histories together with the regional histories of the native peoples of West Africa and America. But Atlantic history is not additive; it is more than the sum of its parts. It is as much Spanish as British, as much Dutch as Portuguese, as much African as American. Second, the assumption that formal, legal structures reflect reality. There are formal designs everywhere in this early modern world—designs for national, mercantilist economic policies, for the administration of governments, imperial, regional, and local, and for the principles and institutions of organized religion. But rarely do these formal designs reflect reality. Beneath the formal structures lies the informal actuality, which has patterns of its own.[3]

The starting point, it seems to me, is to recognize the impossibility of defining any specific set of characteristics that carries through the entire three centuries of the Atlantic world in the early modern period. This was no static historical unit whose elements and essential nature lie motionless before the historian. Atlantic history is the story of a world in motion. Its dominant characteristics shifted repeatedly. The problem is not to lump together the whole of the Atlantic world in the early modern period in order to describe in abstract terms its persistent strata, its layers. The task, I believe, is the opposite: to describe not the abstracted, meta-historical structural elements but the phasing of the development of this world, its motion and dynamics—to grasp its history as process.[4]

It will not easily be done. The Atlantic world was multitudinous, embracing the people and circumstances of four continents, countless regional economies, languages, and social structures, beliefs as different as Dutch Calvinism and Inca sun worship, and ethnicities as different as those of Finland's Saamis and Africa's Igbos. The variations, as John Elliott has written, are enormous: variations in the European backgrounds of settlers in the Western Hemisphere, variations in types of settlers, variations in settlement environments and native cultures, variations in attitudes, ambitions, and ideals.[5] A uniform chronology across the entire area cannot be expected, nor neat divisions in time; and in an effort to find patterns in this multicultural history one runs the risk of exaggerating similarities and parallels unrealistically. Yet in the evolution of this protean world there was, I believe, despite all the complexities, at least in rough terms, a common morphology, a general overall pattern, however fluid and irregular, of development and change—a pattern that transcends and subsumes the familiar stories of national rivalries for primacy in the Atlantic: Spain's conquests and hegemony in the sixteenth century, partly shared with Portugal; the successful challenges to Spain's dominance in the seventeenth century by the English, Dutch, and French; the bitter struggles for supremacy among the northern Atlantic powers; and Britain's ultimate emergence as the dominant economic and colonizing power and the triumphant naval and military power as well. Equally familiar are the specific histories of the European settlements in America and the massive, forced diaspora of the West African people. But there is a history of another order—a broader, more general and inclusive history, Atlantic in its essence—whose passages were common to all of these manifest events and to all of the variant circumstances in Europe, Africa, and America.

I

In its first, original phase Atlantic history in the broadest sense is the story of the creation of a vast new marchland of European civilization, an ill-defined, irregular outer borderland, thrust into the world of indigenous peoples in the Western Hemisphere and in the outer reaches of the British archipelago. Life in this contested marchland was, literally, barbarous: that is, in its initial stages it was, in large areas, a scene of conflict with alien people, alien in language and mores, hostile in purpose, savage and uncultivated. Europeans, native Americans, and displaced Africans, all—each from their own point of view—saw it that way. For all, others were intent on destroying the civility—European, native American, African—that had once existed. Latin America, to paraphrase John Elliott, was no wilderness; the conquest made it that.[6]

The emerging marchlands, north and south, were scenes of savage wars, wars of conquest and resistance fought with a level of violence that veterans of European wars had not seen before. The European wars of religion and the Thirty Years' War were famous for the devastation they wrought over large areas, but the atrocities in Europe were for the most part limited to defined situations: to assaults on conquered towns that had refused surrender, to provisioning starving troops. Rampaging soldiers could not always be controlled, especially when enflamed with confessional fears and hatreds, and frenzied mobs could wreak terrible devastation, as could the subsequent forces of repression. But authorized brutality when it occurred was essentially strategic: to assert authority, to compel conformity, to terrorize by example, not to commit physical or cultural genocide.[7]

Warfare in the Atlantic marchlands was different, characterized by authorized brutality without restraint, scorched-earth campaigns, the exuberant desecration of the symbols of civility.

The colonial wars were as barbaric, as genocidal, on the part of the English and Dutch as on the part of the Spanish. If Las Casas exaggerated the cruelty of the rampaging conquistadors ("great massacres, burning alive and running through with swords countless innocent victims") the chroniclers of the English and Dutch invaders did not. Hard-bitten English war veterans—"hammerours," Richard Hakluyt called them—were sent to Virginia after the massacre of the English settlers in 1622 for the specific purpose of wiping these "rude, barbarous, and naked people" off the face of the earth. It was, English officials wrote, "a perpetual war without peace or truce"—a project of extermination in which the conquerors were largely successful. Just as the Spanish, according to Las Casas, "took infants from their mothers' breasts, snatching them by the legs and pitching them headfirst against the crags or . . . threw them into the rivers," so English raiders, the Earl of Northumberland's son reported, after throwing Powhatan's children into the water "and shooting out their brains," stabbed their mother to death as a merciful alternative to burning her alive.[8] Torture and dismemberment were practiced on both sides, as settlers and natives alike sought not merely to defeat the enemy but, as Joyce Chaplin has written, to destroy their humanity, to reduce them to mere matter.[9] The Dutch were no less brutal. After a hundred unsuspecting Indians were killed in raids near New Amsterdam—some of the children "cut in pieces before the eyes of their parents," a contemporary wrote, "and the pieces thrown into the fire or into the water"—the few who escaped suffered "the loss of a hand, others of a leg, others . . . holding in their bowels with their hands, and all so cut, hacked and maimed, that worse could not be imagined." Dutch soldiers, who burnt entire village populations alive, used native skulls, it was said, as footballs.[10]

In such an environment the mobilization of a labor force of enslaved Africans—seized initially by Africans, wrenched from their homelands, then organized by Europeans for transport by the thousands, the tens and hundreds of thousands, and pitched into devastating work regimes where often it was found more profitable to work them to death and replace them than to maintain them for long-term service—none of this was unique in its barbarity.[11] All of it was consistent with the exploitative squalor of the settlement years everywhere, north as well as south, among Protestants as well as Catholics. Puritan New England was not different from Mexico or Peru. "It was a fearful sight," the pious, gentle Pilgrim leader William Bradford wrote of New England's Pequot War (1637), "to see [the Indians] frying in the fire and the streams of blood quenching the same, and horrible was the stink and scent thereof." To which the Puritans' military commander added that there were "so many souls . . . gasping on the ground, so thick, in some places, that you could hardly pass along."[12]

And as for that other, nearer, Atlantic frontier—that fa-

mous island in the Virginian sea, as Fynes Moryson called
Ireland in 1617—the Elizabethans, in their struggle to
control the island, slaughtered entire "segments of the na-
tive Irish population," attempting to preserve, in Nicholas
Canny's words, "oases of civility in a desert of barba-
rism." It was a vision in part derived from their knowledge of Spanish and Portuguese experiences in America.
For they were avid readers of the Iberian epics of the New
World, many conveniently translated in compendia like
Richard Eden's *Decades of the Newe World or West India*
(1555, 1577), a 460-page collection of Spanish, Italian, and
Portuguese sources on the early discoveries, explorations,
cultural encounters, and settlements in America. And, as
Jorge Cañizares-Esguerra has shown in great detail, despite all their demonizing of Catholicism, the English
shared with the Spanish the belief that the New World was
the domain of Satan, its people, flora, and fauna permeated
with Satanic depravity, awaiting Christian redemption. A
common European pool of knowledge had developed,
Canny writes, about the processes and consequences of
colonization and exploitation: "authors of whatever nationality and religion . . . drew upon the same authorities
to justify their involvement in actions that were morally
dubious."[13]

Thus Edward Waterhouse, in celebrating the revenge
massacre of the Virginian natives in 1622, drew heavily
on—quoted directly from—Fernández de Oviedo's *General and Natural History of the Indies . . .* (1535, 1557),
which extolled Cortés's brutal conquest of Mexico, citing
volume and chapter of Oviedo's description of the Indi-

ans' idleness, viciousness, melancholy, childishness, stupidity, and guile.[14] His uncle, Sir Edward Waterhouse, shared with his patron, Sir Henry Sidney, the Lord Deputy of Ireland, who was familiar with the Spanish subjugation of indigenous peoples, a parallel view of the Irish as "more uncivil, more uncleanly, more barbarous and more brutish in their customs . . . than in any other part of the world."

There was a widespread mutuality of experience. Sidney's sanctioning of the indiscriminate killings at Mullaghmast, Kildare, in 1578 would find its parallel in the authorized Anglo-Indian wars in the Chesapeake, just as the Earl of Essex's slaughter of six hundred unarmed men, women, and children on Ireland's Rathlin Island in 1574 would be duplicated in the killings at Mystic, Connecticut, six decades later. There might not be an *exact* North American equivalent to Sir Humphrey Gilbert's reported treatment of the defeated Irish—placing their severed heads on "each side of the way leading into his own tent so that none could come [to see him] but . . . he must pass through a lane of heads, [which terrorized] the people when they saw the heads of their dead fathers, brothers, children, kinsfolk, and friends lie on the ground before their faces, as they came to speak with the said colonel."[15] But there are similarities enough. As part of the colonists' devastating revenge massacre in Virginia in 1622 one Capt. Daniel Tucker, sent ostensibly to conclude peace with the Patawomeke Indians, toasted the armistice with poisoned wine that killed, it was said, some two hundred of the assembled natives, then circled back to kill fifty who survived, bringing home with him "part[s] of their heads" as trophies.[16]

The obverse has parallels too. There were always among the Europeans, English as well as Spanish and Portuguese, advocates of the indigenous Americans' humanity and civility, men who sought to understand and explain the natives' civilization, to preserve their well being, and to establish peaceful relations between the races—Bartolomé de Las Casas, José de Acosta, António Vieira, Thomas Harriot. But their expressed concerns were polemical or theoretical, and at best only marginally effective in the practical world of remorseless exploitation and fear-driven belligerence.[17]

The bloody conflicts and the demoralization that resulted, involving as much the English, Dutch, and French as the Spanish, formed an ever-present reality, something most people in the areas of contact, native and European alike, either experienced themselves or knew about. They permeated everyday existence, penetrated ordinary awareness, and formed the core of the general sense that this was a world in which the normal rules of civility, native American or European, were suspended, and human relations were reduced to atavistic conflicts.

The barbarousness of the initial European conquests from Hudson Bay to Patagonia is part of a more general condition of life in these early years. For much of a century—two or three generations—everything in the areas of contact and settlement in the Western Hemisphere was fluid, indeterminate, without stable structures or identities. Possession had no fixed meaning. Territorial claims were unreliable, often ignored when known, and commonly contested.

In the course of the seventeenth century possession of the tiny Caribbean island of St. Kitts changed hands between the French and English seven times before, in 1713, almost a century after the first settlements, the island finally became officially and permanently English. Similarly Tobago, settled in 1628 by the Dutch, "was occupied alternately and sometimes simultaneously, by English, French, Dutch, and Courlandian [Latvian] colonists" until finally, after fifty years of struggle, it was taken over by the French. Curaçao was Spanish, then Dutch. Dutch New Netherlands, which had absorbed Sweden's colony on the Delaware River, was itself taken by the English in 1664, then retaken by the Dutch a decade later before being permanently recovered by the English. Brazil was Portuguese, then for twenty-four years largely Dutch, then Portuguese again. When in 1624 a group of Walloons ventured to Guyana, then accurately called the Wild Coast, between the Amazon and Orinoco deltas, they found there English, French, Irish, Spanish, Portuguese, and Dutch traders, colonizers, and adventurers claiming then losing and sometimes regaining possession of parcels of land and trading sites. It was a scene of devastation: squalid settlements, abandoned shelters, burnt-out forts, and ragged survivors of jungle raids and small battles seeking some kind of security. The struggles were continuous, almost formless. Some involved groups of Indians loosely associated with Spanish and Portuguese soldiers bent on driving out the English, Dutch, and Irish; others consisted of ragtag English raiders attempting to beat off the Spanish, who were at the same time subject to assaults by the Dutch. Though the Dutch managed to keep control of trading stations on Surinam, Essequibo, and Berbice, there was little public authority in these ramshackle, polyglot, disease-ridden settlements; when it appeared, it was fragile and temporary. Elsewhere, similarly, possession shifted, and national allegiances blurred. The acting governor of the Dutch, formerly Swedish, colony on the Delaware River, fresh from warfare in Brazil, declared that if the Dutch authorities did not properly support him he would turn the place over to the English, Portuguese, Swedes, or Danes—"What the devil did he care," he was quoted as saying, "whom he served?"[18]

It was a time, throughout the Western Hemisphere, of pervasive social disorder and disorientation.[19] On the British Caribbean islands before 1713 there were seven major slave revolts—major, in that more than fifty slaves were involved and in which both blacks and whites were killed—and six that were cut off early in the planning stage. An incipient uprising on Barbados in 1675 resulted in the execution, by burning, hanging, and beheading, of thirty-five negroes before the tumult subsided.[20] Indentured servants were no less rebellious. As early as 1629 they turned on their masters on Nevis, and swam out to greet the Spanish invaders crying "Liberty, joyfull Liberty." Irish servants—who had swarmed onto the islands (fully a third of the entire white population of the English Leeward Islands were Irish in 1678) and who were despised and brutalized by their English masters—led the way in a series of violent protests. In 1692 their plot, in collaboration with creole slaves, to overwhelm Barbados planters and take over the island resulted in ninety-two executions, four deaths from castration, and eighteen deaths from other causes. At one point they joined with the French in assaults on the British.[21]

In the new borderlands—new at different times and places—civility was lost in a world of turmoil. Life in seventeenth-century "Amazonia" (northern Brazil), where Europeans of seven nations struggled with natives, was "unstable and social identities . . . unpredictable, fluid and hybrid"; the whole area of contact was a "linguistic cauldron involving Irish, English, Dutch, French, Portuguese, Spanish and 'Gypsy' migrants, as well as the communities of Arawak, Gê and Tupi speakers." Through much of that century English Jamaica, "founded in blood," was a staging area for buccaneers and England's most lawless colony: the Sodom of the Indies, it was called, "the Dunghill of the Universe," according to Ned Ward, "populated exclusively by prostitutes, convicts, and drunks."[22] The key Panamanian links between Spain's Caribbean islands and the Pacific coast, Portobelo and Nombre de Dios, were described as "tropical pest-holes . . . hot, sickly shanty towns" until the fleets arrived, and then became scenes of wild brawling and violent gambling. In New Netherland the trading season was a time of uproar, as ruthless traders ambushed the arriving Indian fur trappers, bribed them, robbed them, and beat them. Marketing became a frenzy, gambling became wild, magistrates were assaulted, and drunken women, native and Dutch, joined in the brawls and roamed the streets until they were thrown into make-shift jails. Everywhere, even in the apparently tranquil areas, the received, stable ordering of human relations came under great pressure, weakened, and often failed.[23]

This was a barbarous world for all the people involved, native Americans, Europeans, and Africans alike, struggling for survival with outlandish aliens, rude people, uncivilized people, uncultured in what mattered. All three peoples—native Americans, Europeans, and Africans—felt themselves dragged down into squalor and savagery. All struggled somehow to cling to, to restore, the civility they had once known—some in slave quarters that followed African architectural forms and whose people maintained African kinship ties, languages, magic, music, and dance; some in New England villages shaped to ideals of English local ways; others in cities that partly replicated Spain's distinctive urban spaces; still others on tobacco farms whose owners self-consciously modeled themselves on the English gentry despite the impossibility of duplicating on slave estates the lives of traditional *rentiers.* And when existence could not be kept "literally the same," James Lockhart writes of Latin American society, "whatever was susceptible of treatment on analogy was so treated."[24] Such efforts were instinctive—the urge to escape a disorienting world by clinging to what could be recalled of the familiar, civilized past.

So, Ida Altman tells us in an illuminating account of cultural transmission and retention, emigrants from the town of Brihuega, not far from Guadalajara and Madrid, preserved in New Spain's second city, Puebla de los Angeles, what they could of their "distinctive traditions and identity"—the "social ties and patterns of economic activity familiar to them"—maintaining the "Brihuega-Puebla nexus" as long as they could while struggling to adjust to a world that differed in fundamental ways from what they had known before.[25] And Richard Dunn has vividly described the emulative lives of newly rich sugar barons on tropical Caribbean plantations in the late seventeenth century who wore stifling skirted coats in the latest style, thick waistcoats, showily ribboned knee breeches, at times leather gloves and high boots, while their women suffered in layers of petticoats, stiff corsets, and heavily embroidered cloaks, both men and women shaded by elaborately ornamented hats.[26]

These, in the years of early encounters, were common experiences on the outer marchlands, north and south. But their consequences were not limited to the Western Hemisphere.

Of Europe's reaction to the New World in the sixteenth century—complex, selective, irregular, shifting—John Elliott has written with subtlety and acute penetration. "In observing America [Europe] was, in the first instance, observing itself—and observing itself in one of two mirrors, each of which distorted as it revealed"—the mirror of its own, ideal past of prelapsarian innocence, or the mirror of its presumed actual past, when Europe too had been barbarian in manners and religion. Yet Europe's values and beliefs were "sufficiently rich, diversified, and sometimes self-contradictory to leave space for the partial and relatively painless incorporation of new facts and impressions into an image of the world and of mankind that was neither rigid nor entirely exclusive."[27] Into these interstices, by the late sixteenth century, there flowed a multitude of vivid, often fanciful and polemical accounts in several languages of America's people, its wonders, and the savagery of the conquest. Las Casas's most searing tract, *The Most Brief Account of the Destruction of the Indies,* in which he described, province by province, how the Spanish murdered, tortured, and burnt their way through the world of gentle, defenseless Indians, was published in 1552; by 1600 it had been republished in Flemish, French, English, German, and Latin, with an Italian translation soon to follow. By then knowledge of America, with all its strangeness, and the Spanish conquest, with all its barbarities, had spread widely, though with complex effect, through the literate publics of western Europe. In this process of dissemination, Dutch writers, removed from the reality of the struggles abroad, prone to identify with the native Americans as victims of their common imperial enemy, and sharing in their nation's great flowering in literature, art, and philosophy, were the central force.

Over the course of the sixteenth and seventeenth centuries, the Dutch read about, wrote about, and otherwise rendered the New World in a spectacular variety of contexts. They described America in copious geographies, histories, and poems; in pamphlets, broadsides, and ballads; in paintings, prints, and maps. Most of all, they incorporated America into their public discourse, such that an *idea* of America—an idea that certainly contrasted with other perceptions of the New World—featured prominently in political debates, economic policies, and imaginative writings of the Republic's Golden Age.

They published editions of the writings of Columbus, of Vespucci, of Cortés—of Gómara (on Mexico), of Zárate (on Peru), of Staden (on Brazil)—and their atlases and maps, printed in quantities for broad distribution, kept up with the latest discoveries.[28]

The Dutch had their special nationalist-political reasons for wanting to paint the most wrenching portraits of the Spanish conquest, detailing, as did William of Orange, how Spain in America had treated the natives like beasts, putting "to death more than twenty million people and made desolate and waste thirty times as much land . . . as the Low Country is, with such horrible excesses and riots." But there were parallel writings in other languages, descriptive if not polemical, portraying native American life and its flora and fauna as bizarre, exotic, fantastic— and none more vivid, none more popular than Thomas Harriot's *Briefe and True Report of . . . Virginia* (1588), which was republished first in Richard Hakluyt's encyclopedic *Principall Navigations* (1589) and then in 1590 in Latin, English, French, and German, as the first part of Theodor de Bry's ten-volume compilation of texts and drawings, *America* (1590–1618).[29]

This outpouring of publications and of popular, often shocking graphics was riveting and challenging. It had the effect, however involuted, of extending the range of the European imagination, stimulating thought on human and physical nature, multiplying options for adventure and entrepreneurship, and in general expanding the horizons and possibilities of everyday life. As in various ways, in different degrees of specificity, much of Western Europe became aware of these distant cultural encounters, many puzzled over their meaning and implications.

Those who saw the positive side of these cultural marchlands—not a world of irredeemable brutes and bizarre circumstances, but an elemental, unencumbered world of naturally innocent if ignoble savages not dissimilar to what Europeans once had been—imagined an environment free of the evils of modernity, open to social renewal and reconstruction, and open too to Christian fulfillment, where in isolation one might build a new Jerusalem.

There is no more dramatic expression of the impact America had on the European imagination in these chaotic years than the utopianism it engendered. Many of Spain's most enlightened thinkers, inspired by the powerful reform movement within the Spanish church, by the deep currents of millenarianism sweeping through Iberia, and by the remarkable influence of Thomas More's *Utopia*, saw in the New World a providential opportunity, indeed a divine obligation, to establish in those innocent parts the true apostolic Kingdom of God.[30]

It took many forms. In Mexico, while the secular cleric and audiencia judge Vasco de Quiroga established ideal

Indian communities explicitly modeled on More's vision,[31] Franciscan friars located the natives' existence at a critical juncture in the approach to the Apocalypse and "assigned them a primordial, privileged role at the center . . . of the future of humanity." Native Mexican society, at least before the Aztecs' conquest, they explained in their chronicles, had been pristine, peaceful, and well ordered. It had lacked the curse of private ownership and had been free of luxury, greed, and the murderous passion for "rank and honors." So, providentially, the natives themselves had reached the perfect preparatory stage for the advent of the millennium, save for their ignorance of Christianity. The friars therefore struggled to convert the natives to the true religion, by force if necessary, and to help them preserve their pre-Aztec innocence. And they did what they could to isolate them from Spanish influences—just as the Jesuits would do in their strictly disciplined theocratic "reductions" of the Guaraní in Paraguay—so that they might fulfill their millenarian promise. Inevitably they, like the Jesuits, clashed with royal authority and their efforts were forcibly suppressed. But their dream of a Mexican-Christian utopia, conceived in the monasteries of Spain and in their American missions, lingered on and reached high places. The greatest of the Franciscan utopians, Friar Toríbio Motolinía, lectured the emperor Charles V on his obligation, in what the friar called this "supreme moment for humanity," to hasten the coming of the Final Judgment by freeing the Franciscans to help the natives recover their lost, quasi-apostolic innocence.[32]

The millenarian hopes of various Protestant utopians were no different. The parallels are striking: "eschatological convictions supplied a profound dimension to Puritan life. They filled sermons and commentaries, colored diaries, martyrologies, and even poetry, and sometimes determined life decisions at the most personal level." For the Puritans, New England's congregationalism—the gathering of the elect—was in itself a sign of the approaching millennium. Their greatest theologian, John Cotton, "a prophet of the coming glory," devoted his Thursday sermons to predicting the imminent transition to saintly power and the universal empire of the Lord, while lesser preachers attempted to fix the exact moment when the Saints' Fifth Monarchy would appear.

But it was the Reverend John Eliot, enflamed by readings in Revelation and Ezekiel, rejoicing in the fevered millenarianism of Interregnum England, and convinced that the Indians were the lost Hebrews about to return to the Lord, who took the most practical steps to advance the Lord's approaching dominion. The isolated Indian praying towns he founded were designed as models for global replication in anticipation of the Second Coming. Convinced that the destruction of the Stuart monarchy in 1649 had made England "*the* inaugural location for the millennium," in his main publication, *The Christian Commonwealth,* he urged England to adopt his praying towns as prototypes for the emerging "Kingdom of the Lord Jesus." In 1660 his Fifth Monarchy preachings ("Christ is the only right heir of the Crown of England") were an embarrassment to the restored government of Charles II, just as the Franciscans' had been to the government of Charles V; and in anticipation of the Crown's wrath, the Massachusetts authorities confiscated and destroyed every copy of Eliot's treatise they could get hold of and forced the prophet to disown everything in it.[33]

Eliot was but one of many Protestant utopians who, frustrated in Europe, saw in the barbarous American borderlands the ultimate site for their perfect communities. Pilgrims, Mennonites, Quakers, Rosicrucians, Labadists, Moravians, Amish, Dunkards, Schwenkfelders—all projected their evangelical passion for apostolic purity, ignited in the spiritually burnt-over districts of Europe, into what they considered to be pristine sites in the New World. And none more fervently, or more fatally, than the Dutchman Pieter Cornelius Plockhoy.

With his friends, the freethinkers and poets in Amsterdam's "Sweet Rest" tavern, Plockhoy designed, in the 1640s, a model community, to be replicated across the globe—a community of perfect equality, absolute toleration, and mutual sharing in all things—a communistic welfare society where people would contribute what they could and take what they needed. Exhilarated by this exalted vision, Plockhoy sought to realize his dream first in stolid Holland; then, when that failed, in England, where, with the help of that tireless, all-purpose reformer Samuel Hartlib, he managed to present his case personally to Cromwell. When the Lord Protector died he turned to the Archbishopric of Cologne, where Dutch Mennonite influences had been strong. There too he found no support for his plans. And so finally Plockhoy withdrew, with a small band of disciples, to an abandoned clearing on the Delaware River called Whorekill, where, in 1664, the community he had designed to transform life on earth was wiped out by the conquering English—wiped out, it was officially reported, "to a very naile."[34]

But it was in Pennsylvania that the radical messianic utopianism that swept through the Protestant sects—impulses that tended to exhaust themselves in the dense social environment of Europe—bore the most plentiful fruit.

It began with the arrival in 1694 of the learned Transylvanian Johannes Kelpius and his followers, until then known as the Chapter of Perfection. Kelpius was a model Rosicrucian mystic, a magus, and also a *magister* of the University of Altdorf. With his followers, he built just outside Philadelphia, on a ridge overlooking a creek, a log-walled monastery where the brethren could search for perfection in trancelike states by contemplating their magic numbers and their esoteric symbols. In a primitive laboratory they conducted chemical and pharmaceutical experiments aimed at eliminating disease and prolonging life indefinitely. And on the roof they built a telescope, which they manned from dusk till dawn, so that in case, as they put it, the Bridegroom came in the middle of the night, their lamps would be prepared—which is to say, they would be prepared to receive the expected Deliverer. But the heart of Kelpius' sect—which they renamed The Woman in the Wilderness, after a passage in Revelation—

lay not in the common room, not in the cells, not in the laboratory, and not in the rooftop *Sternwarte,* but in a cave which the magus found in a nearby hillside and in which he spent most of his life after his arrival in Pennsylvania pondering a truth concealed to ordinary souls but revealed to him by signs, by symbols, by numbers, and by sheer contemplation. For he knew with certainty that the wilderness into which the Woman in Revelation (the pure church) had fled was Pennsylvania. It was here, he believed, that mankind would "find the dear Lord Jesus"; it was here that the true Christian, vigilantly trimming his lamp, should await the Bridegroom and prepare for the heavenly feast.[35]

II

But in time—different times in different places; there is no neat chronology—the scattered Euro-Afro-American world changed, emerged into a long phase of development and integration. The growth of stability and development was aided by the fact that nowhere was imperial governance, designed abroad, absolute, its mandates uniformly enforced. Everywhere the formal precepts and injunctions were modified, compromised, and redirected in response to the pressures of local situations. "I obey" was the formula of Spanish-American administrators faced with rigid decrees, "but I do not execute."

So, gradually, by an infinity of adjustments, negotiations, and extemporized institutions, the indigenous peoples in the Iberian lands came to terms with the invaders and conquerors—invidiously, as laborers, free and unfree, and tributaries, but also as victors in preserving significant elements of their native cultures within the matrix of Christian civilization. A general language evolved in "Amazonia" that "incorporated the insistent and dynamic linguistic forces of the Portuguese, Tupi, Tupinamba languages . . . linking (Tupi) Indians to Christianity by way of their ancestral language." In the British north the indigenous peoples struggled, in the end unsuccessfully, to sustain a middle ground of cultural accommodation—an effort that did succeed, through the efforts of the regular clergy, in New France. Jamaica, once a brawling, lawless lair of buccaneers, its main port a nest of brothels and taverns and its backcountry a scattering of frontier farms and scrabbling ranches, became by the early eighteenth century "a classically proportioned sugar society" beset by social and economic problems but dominated by big planters in control of 55,000 slaves and closely linked by fixed trade routes to Britain and the main lines of Atlantic commerce. North and south, stable communities were built and flourished: in the north substantial port towns and secure networks of plantations and farming villages; in the south cities that formed "the general framework of Spanish life." Mexico City and Lima; Bogotá, Guatemala, and Santo Domingo; Panama, Quito, Cuzco, Guadalajara, and Santiago de Chile—all became bastions of Spanish power, in John Womack's phrase, the largest of them, with their Indian hinterlands, the match of all but the greatest European conurbations.[36] National boundaries, though in some places still vague and contested, became more firmly established; some were defined in international law and treaties. No challenges to established territorial claims were successful and sustained from the end of the seventeenth century to the aftermath of the Seven Years' War.[37]

The integration of the once-disordered American marchlands into the emerging Atlantic system was profoundly favored by the ocean's physiography. The clockwise circulation of winds and ocean currents, sweeping westward in the south and eastward in the north and linked by deep riverine routes—the Elbe and Rhine, the Amazon and Orinoco, the Niger and Congo, the Mississippi and St. Lawrence—to immense continental hinterlands, drew the Atlantic into a cohesive communication system. The ocean became, in Chaunu's phrase, an "immutable connection" *("une boucle immuable")* between east and west, or, as the historical geographer Meinig put it, "a single arena of action." Firmly established trade routes joining producers and consumers on both sides of the Atlantic made the ocean a common roadway rather than a forbidding barrier—made the ocean *permeable* space, as Jacques Godechot and Robert Palmer wrote in their essay on Atlantic history—more permeable, more easily traversed in stable routes, than many European land areas.[38]

Mercantilist theories, national rivalries, and nationalist historiography obscure the degree to which a stable pan-Euro-Afro-American economy developed, stretching from central Europe to Britain, Iberia, West Africa, and the Americas, with the Caribbean its western pivot. Despite all the commercial hostilities between rival nations and competitive interests, the pan-oceanic commercial webs that developed as the Atlantic world matured were interwoven, complex, and multitudinous—so complex, so numerous, that they can only be illustrated, not catalogued, enumerated, or fully summarized.

Thus New England, not more than 5 percent of whose population was African, was dependent on the African slave trade for its economic survival since the major markets for its agricultural products were the West Indian slave plantations; and New England was also dependent on Portuguese and Spanish markets for its cargoes of fish, sent to ports in northern Iberia and carried from there on mule-back into remote inland villages.[39] Similarly, North American rice, produced in the Lower South, was marketed "over a vast area stretching from Peru and Argentina to the shores of the Black Sea," with the German states "the center of consumption."[40] Tobacco too, produced in the Upper South, flowed through many channels, shipped and reshipped. Much of the success of the North American tobacco planters, whose product reached consumers from England to the Rhineland and from Stockholm to Marseilles, feeding the fiscs of half of Europe, depended on the Farmers General of France, which in the eighteenth century became "the greatest re-exporter of colonial goods in Europe." Similarly, in the interconnected swirl of Atlantic commerce, London bankers, together with colleagues in Portugal, dominated the slave trade to Brazil, and most merchants in major Brazilian ports were agents for firms financed by Englishmen, and to a lesser extent by other foreigners.[41]

The Atlantic commercial economy in its early modern maturity was polycentric and dynamic. Britain's Atlantic world was far larger and more complex than its formal Atlantic empire. One association of London merchants and Scotch affiliates in the mid-eighteenth century that we know a great deal about dealt in slaves, sugar, tobacco, timber, and provisions. The debts they incurred in opening plantations in Florida were balanced by profits in slave markets in Africa; profits from contracts for supplying bread to the troops in Germany were invested in land deals in the Caribbean; funds derived from sugar production and marketing provided capital for commercial loans.[42] In the pan-Atlantic scope of their enterprises they were not unique among London's merchants, nor were London's merchants unique in conducting multilateral trade. Bristol's "ships and seamen could be found from Labrador to Angola, from Curaçao to the Cape Verde Islands, and from Virginia to Amsterdam"; the city's merchants kept especially close contact with Philadelphia, Jamaica, Newfoundland, and various Caribbean islands. And British merchants, protected by treaties and extraterritorial rights in Lisbon and Oporto, "penetrated the whole fabric of [Portugal's] metropolitan and colonial economy."[43]

The energy, the intensity, of Atlantic commerce, coursing through established channels, soared in the eighteenth century. By mid-century 1,000 ships a year were involved in England's transatlantic traffic, 459 in the sugar trade alone. France in 1773 sent 1,359 ships across the Atlantic to transport colonial goods. No less than 3,500 vessels were engaged annually in the Atlantic wine trade, moving out from six nations—Britain, Denmark, the Netherlands, France, Spain, and Portugal—to the Azores and the Canaries where they took on cargoes for delivery in 104 ports in Europe, Africa, and North and South America. The traffic in this commodity alone formed a complex and stable network—or system of networks. And the Dutch—middlemen, shippers, slavers, planters, and settlers—who for two centuries committed more funds and dispatched more people to Atlantic ventures than to Asian and for whom "Atlantic commerce was . . . far more important than trade with Asia"—created their own pan-Atlantic web of settlements and trade routes. Their immensely profitable commercial entrepôts of Curaçao (a free port after 1675) and St. Eustatius distributed European goods across all mercantilist barriers in the West Indies and mainland South America and reshipped tropical produce and bullion to the Netherlands. At the inner core of their trading operations was a close-woven network of enterprising Sephardic Jews with connections throughout the Atlantic world. Having made up half of the population of Dutch Brazil, they had spread out from there to all the western colonies; by the mid-eighteenth century they comprised one-third of the European population of Curaçao.[44]

But in the first century of colonization and more, it was Spain's commercial economy, empowered by the production and distribution of precious metals, that was the key to the development of the Atlantic system. Formally, Spain's western commercial system, fully in place by the mid-sixteenth century, was a pseudo-mercantilist, Castilian-nationalist monopoly, but in fact by the end of the seventeenth century it was open to and involved with the whole of Europe's economy. For Spain's main economic center in southern Andalusia had failed to develop a goods-producing base, and so it was dependent on other European suppliers to serve the markets of its far-flung western empire, from which flowed in return its great treasures of silver, gold, and exotic commodities. Of necessity, therefore, Spain opened its economy to the most forceful entrepreneurs of Europe. Foreign merchants—British, Genoese, Flemish, French, and Dutch—provided the vital goods through their commission houses in Seville and Cádiz, and thereby acquired control of much of the Spanish Atlantic trading system. "Half of Europe, from Genoa to Hamburg," was involved in the "big business" of exploiting America through Spain's Indies trade. Some 94 percent of the value of all goods shipped to America in Spain's famous convoys of *flotas* and *galeones* in the late seventeenth century consisted of non-Spanish goods; 40 percent of the exports via Cádiz were French in origin. It was a self-intensifying system. As the goods of Europe's advanced economies flooded Spain's American markets, capital increasingly drained from lower Andalusia to England, France, Italy, and the Low Countries, and the returns in silver from Mexico and Peru flowed back through the foreign branch houses in Seville and Cádiz to irrigate the whole of Europe's economy. American silver, Stanley and Barbara Stein write, in exchange for the manufactures of Holland, Flanders, England, France, Italy, and Germany, "was a major (perhaps even the determining) factor in the development of commercial capitalism in western Europe." It seems perverse, a Flemish scholar has written, that the more passive Lower Andalusia's role in Atlantic commerce became, the more it stimulated Europe's economy. Thus Pufendorf: "Spain kept the cow and the rest of Europe drank the milk."[45]

What made all this possible—what helped bind the widespread and intensely competitive Atlantic commercial world together—was the mass of illegal trade that bypassed the formal, nationalistic constraints. Much of Europe's exploitation of Spain's American empire rested on smuggling, on corruption, on fraud of all kinds, the magnitude of which, though less than British and French legal exports to their metropoles, created in effect a parallel economy independent of the official system. "Official corruption" of Spain's commercial system, the Steins write, "became an imperative of survival." There were not simply leakages in the formal system but open sluices. So massive was the under-registration of goods exported by the European commission houses in Spain, "so extraordinarily fraudulent," writes Michel Morineau, that "it was no longer fraud." Spain's attempts in later years to constrict the volume of smuggling would lead to bristling diplomacy with France and, in 1739, to war with Britain.[46]

But this clandestine multinational plundering of one nation's commerce by aggressive competitors was not something unique to Spain's Atlantic economy. Everywhere illegal connections brought together people and economies otherwise separated. Nothing the Brazilian or Portuguese authorities could do could stop the smuggling from the gold fields of Minas Gerais to Portugal, England, and Africa. Illegal gold sales became so common, despite two dozen decrees forbidding the trade, that smugglers could count on regular commissions above normal profits. The Dutch stronghold at Elmina in West Africa became such a hub of this illicit trade that return voyages arrived in America loaded with miscellaneous European goods, the cost of slaves having failed to consume the profits of the gold sales. The major Brazilian ports—Rio de Janeiro, Salvador, Pernambuco—as well as such smaller inlets as Santa Catarina and Paratí, were flooded with foreign merchandize, in part because of the work of companies in faraway Liverpool and London that had been organized for the specific purpose of invading the Brazilian economy.[47]

So too French sugar products were smuggled into British North American territory with the indulgence if not the encouragement of corrupt customs officials. In some places manuals were printed that listed the standardized bribes. The situation in the North American ports was similar to that of Cádiz, where too the "legitimization of fraud" took the form of standardized payoffs—regular, reliable commissions for needy aristocrats willing to pass packages of silver and gold over the city walls—and so much per bale for tidewaiters who ignored the unloading of unregistered goods. In Massachusetts the magnitude of the illegal trade in French Caribbean sugar products, which flooded the North American markets, is suggested by the fact that in 1754–1755 only 384 hogsheads of molasses were officially entered in the port of Boston while 40,000 hogsheads per year were needed to keep the province's sixty-three distilleries going, none of which ceased operation. It was largely this illegal trade with the French islands, facilitated by universal "compounding" by customs officials, that made possible a positive balance of payments in the face of a severely negative balance of legal trade; and it was the effort to root out that deeply embedded clandestine trade that led to the Writs of Assistance case, the first act of the American Revolution.[48] Spain's shipments of European goods in its elaborate semi-annual convoys were regularly smuggled from Cuba into all the adjacent areas, and smugglers also swarmed through Spanish American trade routes from Dutch bases in Curaçao, British bases in Jamaica, and French bases in Hispaniola. Smuggling was "almost [the] raison d'être" of the Dutch Antilles. Antigua was "a smuggler's paradise," and "the French, Dutch, and English used the *asientos* [the Spanish slave contracts] as a front for all sorts of illegal deals with the Spanish Caribbean."[49]

And what was once clandestine, if routine, could in time become legally sanctioned. Spain granted limited contracts to Portuguese, French, and British poachers, and in the Treaty of Utrecht in 1713 officially transferred the entire slave *asiento* to the British, along with a window (the annual "permission" ship) into the empire's general trade. Though the contract itself, in the hands of the disastrous South Sea Company during a period of constant warfare, proved to be unprofitable, it contributed to Britain's overwhelming success as the premier supplier of slaves to the entire Western Hemisphere.[50] In the course of the eighteenth century, ships from Liverpool, Bristol, and London delivered 2.5 million Africans (40 percent of that century's total) to slave markets throughout North, Central, and South America.[51] How complex Britain's slave trade was, how tightly bound into the lives and work of people on four continents, has been shown in detail by Stephen Behrendt. One can now see how the trade proceeded through carefully timed transaction cycles involving goods producers in Britain and northern Europe; slave marketers in Africa; and labor jobbers, planters, and ordinary consumers throughout the Americas. The dovetailing of far-flung transaction sequences, the close matching of supply and demand in the face of incomplete and inaccurate knowledge of available goods and markets, was intricate and cunningly contrived. A single misjudgment or accident in mobilizing trading goods and in anticipating the supply of slaves in Africa and the labor markets in the Americas could spell economic disaster.[52]

The elements of the Atlantic world in these years were integrated not only economically, but socially, culturally, and demographically. The Europeans in the Western Hemisphere were not parasitic as they were in the Far East—"microscopic," in P. J. Marshall's words, "on the fringes of the great Asian empires." There, in India and Indonesia, where the Spanish and Portuguese had been trading by sea from the early years of the sixteenth century and where the Dutch and English would follow, the ancient civilizations, "densely populated and firmly governed, did not suffer the incursions of foreigners easily." Until the late eighteenth century, native merchants controlled trade, manufacturing was managed in Asian terms, Asian rulers controlled the potent land forces, and the Europeans were never able to control the high seas "with the completeness that they dominated the Atlantic." The Americas were different. Starting in sparsely inhabited coastal areas the Europeans built not factories, forts, and enclaves of trading communities perched on the margins of exotic territories and dependent on the goodwill and commercial interests of local authorities, but self-sustaining, entrepreneurial settler societies of mixed European, native American, and African peoples. Their presence deepened and radiated out into the continental interiors, pressing into and reshaping indigenous societies, creating new forms of economic and social life. The Iroquois peoples on the shores of North America's Great Lakes were as much affected as the Peruvian natives on the shores of Lake Titicaca.[53]

The later Atlantic world can be conceived of as, in effect, an immensely complex and regionally differentiated

Euro-Afro-American labor system. When tobacco and sugar prices rose in European markets, production expanded in plantations 3,000 miles away, new areas of cultivation were opened up, and the need for plantation labor, slave and free, increased accordingly. Generation after generation England's exported undesirables proved to be highly desirable additions to the productive American work force: Puritans under Laud, vagrants under the early Stuarts, prisoners of war under Cromwell, Quakers under the later Stuarts, and convicts by the thousands—an estimated total of 50,000—under the Hanoverians. In all, from England, Scotland, and Ireland some 700,000 people migrated to the Atlantic colonies before the Revolutionary era. Though the Spanish had the advantage of a socially disciplined native labor force in America that was huge and reliable even after decimation by disease and war, and though immigration from Spain was formally restricted to those "pure of blood" to the second generation, the Spanish too drew to the Atlantic colonies significant numbers of immigrants, perhaps 688,000 in all— some ambitious family groups seeking economic opportunities, some younger sons and marginal *hidalgos,* but mainly indigent laborers, tradesmen, farm workers, undesirables (Jews, Muslims, and Protestants who slipped through the bureaucracy), and a very large number of undocumented soldiers and sailors. French Canada drew fewer from the homeland—perhaps 70,000, many of whom returned—emigrants not from the countryside but from the modernizing, cosmopolitan towns and cities in the coastal regions and the districts around Paris; those who were of rural origins came from "regions that were well integrated into market economies, and where agriculture was incipiently capitalist." The French islands drew many more, for a possible gross total of 375,000 French Atlantic emigrants before 1760. And almost everywhere in the Atlantic colonies there were scatterings of Dutch, Irish, and Scotch.[54]

But it was of course from Africa that by far the largest number of workers were drawn to the Western Hemisphere: a total of over 5.5 million by 1775—36 percent to British America, 32 percent to Portuguese territory, 13 percent to French territory, 9 percent to Spanish. Enslaved and distributed by a pan-Atlantic, Afro-European coercive commercial system, they were people whose presence almost everywhere in the Western Hemisphere was a major demographic, social, and economic force—in some places (St. Domingue, South Carolina) an overwhelming force. Everywhere, in time, their initially indeterminate legal status became formulated, differently at different times in different places, and everywhere full of ambiguities derived from the impossibility of consistently treating people as things, but officially articulated in each case. And everywhere they were at the heart of the Atlantic "system," fundamental to the entire Atlantic economy. It was slavery, Barbara Solow writes,

> that made the empty lands of the western hemisphere valuable producers of commodities and valuable markets for

Europe and North America: What moved in the Atlantic in these centuries was predominantly slaves, the output of slaves, the inputs of slave societies, and the goods and services purchased with the earnings on slave products . . . Slavery thus affected not only the countries of the slaves' origins and destinations but, equally, those countries that invested in, supplied, or consumed the products of the slave economies.[55]

Information as well as trade and people moved in stable routes, which in their entirety formed a communication system that, however erratically, bound Peru to Seville, Rio de Janeiro to Lisbon, Appalachia to Ireland, Scotland to Barbados, the Rhineland to Pennsylvania. The interpenetrations were deep. The lives of peasants in obscure Basque communities in the western Pyrenees were transformed by their contact with the New World. Events on the other shores of the Atlantic drew men from Basque valleys into the Spanish American colonies and plantations, and their impact on their original homeland "ended up creating a new local gentry based on colonial riches and transatlantic networks. The Indies . . . gave Basques from Oiartzun and other places a unique opportunity to redefine their place and mission as an organic component of the Spanish monarchy, and to reaffirm their ethnic differences in respect to other Iberian peoples."[56] Similarly, though France had fewer ties to the Western Hemisphere through emigration than Britain, Spain, Ireland, and the southwest German states, the "Atlantic boom" penetrated deeply into the social economies of its remote hinterland. The Atlantic trade drew "flour and wine from the Aquitaine, cloth from Sedan and Languedoc, canvas from western France, lace from Valenciennes or Puy, [and] silk stockings and gloves from Cévennes and Dauphiné." So too the lives of Germans, in remote corners of the Neckar Valley, in Württemberg, and in the Kraichgau, were impacted by ties to their countrymen in North America; and for several generations Scots in isolated homesteads far from the Lowland cities maintained contact with kin and former neighbors who had migrated—or had been exiled—to Nova Scotia, North Carolina, and the West Indies.[57]

Religion played a major role in forming and maintaining these networks. While we have long known of the elaborate structure of the Catholic Church in Spanish America—its far-flung parochial system and the subsystems of regular clergy which together penetrated into all corners of the settled territories and linked them to the hierarchy of the metropolitan Church—we have not as clearly seen the Atlantic networks of the Protestant churches. They too, in different, more diverse ways, spread across and bound together elements of the Euro-American world.

Puritanism in all but its Presbyterian form could allow for no formal hierarchy or central authority, yet through most of the seventeenth century loose, informal but effective connections brought together Puritans of various doctrinal positions in England, New England, Ireland, the Netherlands, and the West Indies. Theological, ecclesiastical, political, and personal information flowed through this North Atlantic network, binding these scattered co-religionists together for at least three generations. The Mather family, for example, with members in all five locations, formed in itself an effective late seventeenth-century Atlantic communication system, as did the Winthrops in earlier years.[58]

The hierarchical structure of the Anglican Church embraced all of the British territories; and, though it never established an Episcopal seat in America, through the authority of the Bishop of London it maintained ties throughout the empire and extended its gospel mission through its Society for the Propagation of the Gospel in Foreign Parts. By 1785 the Society had sent out 353 agents or missionaries to more than 200 American locations and maintained an elaborate correspondence with its delegates from its central office in London. But, paradoxically, it was the Quakers, severely antihierarchical in doctrine, who of all the English created the most perfectly integrated and well-disciplined pan-Atlantic religious organization. From the start they looked abroad from their hearth in northern England and sent out their missionaries in all directions—to the Low Countries, the German states, Scandinavia, France, and Italy—and above all to the British colonies in the Western Hemisphere. In five short years, 1655–1660, they established beachheads in every one of Britain's Atlantic colonies, and they forged a system of bonds "which held them tightly together over the vast area." The key to their bonding was less the web of associated meetings they created—monthly, quarterly, yearly—which multiplied with the spread and increase of their population, than their "itinerant ministry." "The bloodstream of the transatlantic Society of Friends," they coursed through their transoceanic network year after year. The traveling ministers—male and female: any approved person could travel on the Quakers' business— made possible a remarkable degree of uniformity in doctrine and practice in communities scattered across thousands of miles of land and ocean and created a vivid sense of the sect's brotherhood and sisterhood. By 1700 nearly 150 men and women had crossed the ocean on such missions, many remaining in passage for two or three years "unifying and solidifying the Quaker community." One itinerant testified in the early eighteenth century to having traveled 21,000 miles to visit 480 meetings. Rebecca Larson has identified and sketched the careers of 57 "transatlantic women" between 1700 and 1775, a subset of the 356 American Quaker women ministers whom she lists in her *Daughters of Light*.[59]

But the German Protestant sects were also—some equally—effective in maintaining pan-Atlantic ties, and especially in reaching out to the native American peoples. The Moravians—the *Unitas Fratrum*, descendants of the pre-Reformation Hussites whose movement had been renewed at Herrnhut, Saxony—were above all evangelists, determined from their earliest years "to win souls for the Lamb."[60] And win they did. Though their home community at Herrnhut numbered less than a thousand before the American Revolution, they circled the Atlantic world, establishing missions in what, for these east Germans, were the least likely places—London, Ireland, Stockholm, Silesia, Greenland, West Africa, South Africa, Antigua, Tobago, Barbados, the Danish West Indies, Berbice, Paramaribo, Surinam—while spreading out from their main North American settlements in Pennsylvania to the Indian territories of the eastern seaboard.[61] By 1748 they had thirty-one congregations in the mainland colonies, and supported some fifty missionaries to the Indians and itinerant preachers, who ranged from Maine to the Carolinas.[62] All of these missions kept ties with each other through conferences, visits, circulating diaries, and letters, and maintained as close bonds with the governing bodies in Germany as a courier system would allow.[63] The Pennsylvanians among them, quickly overcoming their poverty, devoted the profits of their farms and small industries not only to the scattered missions in the colonies but also to the work of their brethren in Europe, whose welfare they considered to be their own.

But the best-organized and most sophisticated of the German-Atlantic evangelicals were the Lutheran Pietists in Halle, near Leipzig, organized by the gifted preacher and administrator August Hermann Francke. By the late seventeenth century they had established links to philanthropic and reform groups in several Imperial Cities and to like-minded organizations in London, particularly the Church of England's Society for the Propagation of Christian Knowledge. Through their intricate network,

"connect[ing] the English movements of charity and educational reform to the North German Pietists and their as-
sociates in commerce and the nobility," they managed the
transfer of persecuted German Protestants, especially exiles from Salzburg, to enclaves in North America, where
they had the protection of the British Crown. An elaborate transdynastic and transterritorial Protestant network,
the Pietists' organization reached from the Francke Foundations in Halle—which included a university, an orphan-
age, a hospital, and a center for the production and distribution of pharmaceuticals—to encampments in the forests
of British North America, and it was maintained as se-
curely as were the Jesuits' ties between Rome and the
métis villagers of French Canada. Just as the Halle missionaries bearing both Pietist beliefs and up-to-date publications and medicines from their small university town
fanned out through the British North American colonies
and the Caribbean, so the Jesuits scattered across French
North American territories. By the early eighteenth century over one hundred priests and lay brothers had established thirty Jesuit missions from Quebec to Wisconsin;
later they would penetrate Louisiana and the Ohio Valley,
baptizing, with varying degrees of success, at least 10,000
adult natives.[64]

THERE WERE Atlantic networks everywhere—economic,
religious, social, cultural—and as they matured, they enhanced the fortunes of creole leaders (American-born, of
European ancestry) who became powerful figures in the
Western Hemisphere, linked to, culturally associated with,

the metropolitan centers of commerce, politics, religion, and high culture.

The mid-eighteenth century in New Spain has been called an era of "creole triumphalism"; it was no less so in the rest of Latin America and in British America as well.[65] Long-established creole families intermarried, controlled landed estates—haciendas in New Spain, sugar plantations in the Caribbean, tobacco farms in Virginia and Maryland—and controlled too other productive enterprises—mining, ranching, shipbuilding, iron production, fisheries. Having consolidated their authority by dense networks of kinship and interest—in Latin America having "gained access to the bureaucracy, bargained over taxes, and become part of the various interest groups disputing royal policy"—the creole elites were as powerful in Virginia as they were in Peru, Brazil, and Mexico. Believing themselves to be rightful lords of the land, they dominated the local jurisdictions, and their authority came to be viewed as such a challenge to the survival of imperial control that the metropolitan authorities, British as well as Spanish, sought to exclude them from major administrative posts in the colonies, an effort that created as much resentment in semi-autonomous New England as in emerging Venezuela where the creole patriots claimed ancestral rights derived from the conquistadors.[66]

III

The creoles' successes and their proud sense of independence ushered in a final phase of early modern Atlantic life—again rough in outline and irregular in time. Creole aristocrats were well educated—in the twenty-odd universities in Spanish America, most dominated by Jesuits; in academies, seminaries, and literary clubs in Portuguese America; in nine quasi-university colleges in British North America—and they were well aware in the mid- and late eighteenth century of the urges toward reform coursing through advanced circles in Europe.[67] The elite among them, provincials but worldly wise, caught their own reflections in the mirror of advanced ideas, and what they saw were rich possibilities of life, if not as an independent nation as in British America then as autonomous provinces within a monarchical commonwealth or federation as in Spanish America. When Britain began its reform of colonial administration after the Seven Years' War and Spain launched its "Bourbon reforms," both increasing revenue demands on the colonies, closing loopholes, and imposing new European administrators and rigid regulations on systems whose successes had lain in their flexibility, the creole elites, north and south, saw a regnant world "at home" that was oppressive and self-absorbed—selfish in its rewards and indifferent to its colonial responsibilities. As they began their complex responses, their cultural self-awareness—hitherto incipient and conflicted—grew and took on clearer form. For a long generation and more, into the early nineteenth century, they groped to define their distinctive identities, increasingly conscious of themselves as different, separate peoples.

For the emerging nations of the Americas this was an age of discovery, of self-discovery, as they sought to find their own, unique place in the world—to discover, as Octavio Paz put it, their proper *patria*. So the elites of Guatemala City, "educated in Enlightenment methods and ideas" in their sophisticated University of San Carlos and eloquent in their progressive *Gazeta de Guatemala* ("a university without walls")

> imagined a "patria" with its own customs, territory, language and history, where equality before the law would attack the culture of privilege, and contributors to society could be measured by utility rather than by race . . . or membership in a corporation.

Such emerging ideas, "new to colonial discourse," and even more radical ideas of extending the "public" to include people of color, Indians, and mestizos, were as yet imaginings, compatible with continued association with the Spanish monarchy. But resistance, successful or not, transformed the bearing of these ideas. The resulting struggles weakened the traditional sources of public authority, jolted and loosened long-settled attitudes and beliefs. The grounds of legitimacy shifted. What had once been seen as provincial imaginings could now be seen as attainable goals in a more enlightened, less burdened society.[68]

Circumstances differed—different demographic, ideological, social, and economic conditions shaped different outcomes at different times. Mexico's messianic, ethnically egalitarian insurgency, led first by the secular priest Miguel Hidalgo and then by José María Morelos—"*Pa-*

dres de la Patria" a contemporary called them—and inspired by the Virgin Mary as Our Lady of Guadalupe, drawing "under her banner . . . sap from the very taproot of Mexican nationality," was scarcely the same as British-American patriotism rooted in devotion to an "ancient constitution" of Saxon times and inspired by the martyrs of a Glorious Revolution that had been fought against Catholic absolutism. Nor was Mexico's halting, unplanned path to independence that followed the failure to achieve home rule within the imperial Spanish state and the collapse of Spain's liberal Cádiz constitution of 1812 the same as North America's self-contained, decisive assertion of autonomy. Yet for all the differences within it, the long era of colonial revolutions was a distinctive phase of the Americas' history—and of Atlantic history generally. For independence, however achieved, and the struggle for political reform in the Western Hemisphere were part of the political transformation of metropolitan Europe—"a part," Jaime Rodríguez writes, "of the larger process of change that occurred in the Atlantic world in the second half of the eighteenth and the early nineteenth centuries"—and ultimately part too of the transformation of Africa's relations with the West.[69]

Reformers and reforming plans and programs formed an interactive network that spread across the Atlantic world. Just as fresh, liberating ideas were transmitted to Mexico, Venezuela, and Río de la Plata by such writers as the immensely influential Benedictine Benito Feijóo—a beacon of the French Enlightenment in Spain, devoted to

the new science of Copernicus, Descartes, and Newton
and a savage critic of popular superstitions—so the challenging, quickly developing political ideas of the opposition Whigs in Britain were conveyed to Williamsburg
and Boston by pamphleteers like Trenchard and Gordon.
The extraordinarily learned Mexican Jesuit Francisco
Clavigero was faithful to scholastic principles, but he too
praised Newton along with Bacon, Descartes, and Franklin, while his colleague, the famously erudite Francisco
Alegre, exiled with Clavigero in Italy, knew Locke and
Hobbes ("Lochio" and "Obbés" in Spain) and believed, as
did so many Hispanic thinkers, that the source of sover-
eignty lay in the consent of the governed. They were, in
the Spanish American world, modernists "in their oratory,
literary productions, pedagogical methods . . . and in their
desire to learn modern languages," and they sought to in-
troduce into Mexican intellectual life "a modified Aristo-
telian philosophical cosmology familiar with and strongly
influenced by eighteenth-century sciences with a heavy
emphasis on empirically based critical analysis."[70]

New, challenging ideas formulated in one area were
picked up in others, assessed and absorbed in varying degrees. Despite all the differences between regions and cultures, the similarities at times were striking. Thus: the
crisis

> was essentially political and constitutional in nature. To be
> sure, it was triggered by new or increased taxes. The cen-
> tral issue, however, was who had the authority to levy new

fiscal exactions . . . [and] deeply embedded in the documents . . . is the belief that unjust laws were invalid, and
that inherent in the *corpus mysticum politicum* was the
right to some kind of popular approval of new taxation . . .
The "unwritten constitution" provided that basic decisions were reached by informal consultation between the
royal bureaucracy and the king's colonial subjects. Usually
there emerged a workable compromise between what the
central authorities ideally wanted and what local conditions and pressures would realistically tolerate. The crisis
. . . was, in short, a constitutional clash between imperial
centralization and colonial decentralization.

So writes the historian, not of the British-American rebel-
lion of 1776 but of the Comunero Revolution of New
Granada (Colombia) of 1781.[71]

Bolívar fiercely rejected Francisco Miranda's faith in
Madison's federalism as the basis of a new Venezuelan
state, but he was as devoted as Madison to the teachings of
Montesquieu and knew more than the Virginian about
Rousseau, whose memory he saluted in a visit to Cham-
béry. It was, and could only have been, Bolívar—a true
Atlanticist: born and bred in Caracas and heir to a great
plantation fortune but educated in Europe and steeped in
the writings of the European and North American Enlightenment—who managed to transmute the customary
themes of creole patriotism (so Catholic, so deep in Hispanic lore) into an affirmation of classical republicanism.
European intellectuals and politicians were no less Atlanticist. David Hume, as Emma Rothschild has shown in a

vivid study, fed on information from all over the Atlantic world—its politics, its wars, its environment, its physical and human condition. His life, she writes, "is an interesting illustration . . . of the ways in which the Atlantic world of the 18th century extended far inland, into the interior of provinces and into the interior of individual existence."

> The oceanic world was at the edge of the vision of almost everyone, as it was at the edge of David Hume's vision, in his childhood home in Berwickshire, or in his little room in La Flèche, as he looked towards the Loir, and to the Loire, and to Nantes and the Atlantic.[72]

The flow of ideas—of arresting thinkers like Hume and of constitutional reformers east and west—permeated the Atlantic communities. It is perhaps not strange that the French Declaration of the Rights of Man and Citizen, which had been inspired by Virginia's bill of rights, swept through the Western world and everywhere heightened reform aspirations.[73] Less obvious was the ubiquitous influence of Cesare Beccaria's *On Crime and Punishment*, that brief but potent manifesto of the Milanese avantgarde which inspired reformers not only in Europe and not only in North America, but also, and especially, in Latin America. Even more influential among the Hispanic American revolutionaries were Bentham's early writings, in part derivative of Beccaria and eloquent in advocating colonial independence. They had such an effect on the intelligentsia of Río de la Plata and the revolutionaries of Venezuela that Bolívar, responding to clerical pressures, attempted, unsuccessfully, to ban them from the *colegios* and universities. And among the most pervasive influences coursing through the Atlantic world was the constitutionalism of the new United States.[74]

For the intelligentsia and reform leaders throughout the Atlantic world the constitutional thought and practice that emerged in the United States provided living examples of what might be done in the restructuring of government, of the dangers that might be avoided, of alternatives that might be explored. American constitutionalism was not a model to be mechanically imitated but a reserve of experience that could be drawn on when needed, intermittently, selectively, with emphases that were shaped differently by the distinctive problems of different societies at different stages of transformation.

The North Americans' constitutional ideas were debated everywhere—in France, in the first year of the National Assembly; in England, where they provided a bridge between the cerebral middle-class reform effort of the eighteenth century and the emerging radicalism of the English working class of the nineteenth century; in Brazil, whose insurgent youths, studying at the University of Coimbra, secretly sought out Jefferson for inspiration and advice; in Chile, where the American constitution was considered an "archetype and example" for their own; in Ecuador, where Vicente Rocafuerte, who in exile in Philadelphia had translated the major American state papers, described the Declaration of Independence as a political Decalogue and the United States Constitution as "the only hope of an oppressed people"; in Mexico, where it inspired the federalism of the Constitution of 1824; and finally in France and Germany in 1848 and in Argentina in 1853.[75]

The Latin American struggles for autonomy and independence, amid the blood-stained rubble of imperial rule, would involve turmoil and tragedy almost everywhere before a degree of stability was achieved. But as political separation from the European states proceeded there was, through this distinctive phase of Atlantic history, no cultural dissociation. As Godechot and Palmer pointed out, the long era of political upheaval and reform in Europe and the Americas was a time when the public worlds of Western Europe and the Americas, for all their differences, were especially close, clearly parts of the same distinctive Atlantic culture. If the European and North American Enlightenments were not a cause of the Latin American revolutions, John Lynch writes, they were "an indispensable source from which leaders drew to justify, defend, and legitimize their actions, before, during, and after the revolution." Jaime Rodríguez is more emphatic. Despite all the bloody power struggles in Latin America, despite the fierce disputes between

> monarchists and republicans, centralists and federalists, and parliamentarians and *caudillos,* a liberal, representative, constitutional government remained the political ideal of the Spanish-speaking nations. Indeed, even the *caudillos* and dictators have been forced to acknowledge, at least in principle, the supremacy of the rule of law and the ultimate desirability of civilian, representative, constitutional government.[76]

So black slavery, that most vivid, most persistent, and most deeply embedded product of the barbarous years, would come under attack that condemned it to extinction. It would survive well into the nineteenth century (in Brazil until 1888), but while in all the years before it had seldom been seen as an overwhelming moral problem and a profound anomaly in Christian society, after the Revolutionary era there was never a time when it was *not* seen as such, when it was *not* challenged and reviled as the "abominable crime" Jefferson called it, and *not* understood to be doomed.

But the achievements of political reform would have no easy future, either in Europe or America, nor did they represent a permanent and irreversible triumph. The new United States had the blessings of both rich markets, hence an economic boom, after the war years, and remarkable political stability; the new Spanish American states had neither. Bolívar, in despair in the month before his death as he surveyed the collapse of Latin America's new republics into despotic fiefdoms and anarchic city-states, wrote that the America he knew was ungovernable: "those who serve the revolution plough the sea . . . this country will fall inevitably into the hands of the unrestrained multitudes and then into the hands of tyrants." Yet the ideals he had expressed so eloquently in his, and the Revolutionary generation's, exuberant youth—"the rights of man, the freedom to work, think, speak, and write . . . a government where innocence, humanity, and peace will reign and where equality and freedom will triumph under the rule of law"—these ideals survived, and, however unrealized or even for a time ignored or rejected, have persisted, and continue to unify the cultures of the Atlantic world.[77]

EUROPE AND THE WESTERN HEMISPHERE, profoundly linked to the peoples and cultures of West Africa, have taken different paths in many spheres since the age of the Enlightenment, and in the course of the nineteenth century they became part of a global world system. But in the prior centuries they formed a distinctive regional entity, bearing the indelible imprints of both the settlement era— violent instability, cultural conflict and alienation, racism, and brutal economic dynamism—and the ideals of the later years—self-government, freedom from arbitrary power, and a sense that the world lies open for the most exalted aspirations. It is this—the fusion of exploitative economic force, ruthless but ingenious, oppressive but creative, and the shared idealism of the Enlightenment— that is the ultimate and permanent legacy of Atlantic history in the early modern years.

But the full account of this story—which is not the aggregate of several national histories, but something shared by and encompassing them all—is a tale yet to be told.

Notes

Acknowledgments

Index

Notes

I. The Idea of Atlantic History

1. The Hamburg conference on Atlantic history (1999) resulted in a volume edited by the convener, Professor Horst Pietschmann: *Atlantic History: History of the Atlantic System 1580–1830* . . . (Göttingen, 2002). The papers at the Dutch conference, "The Nature of Atlantic History" (also in 1999), were published as a forum in *Itinerario,* 23, no. 2 (1999). Marcel Dorigny edited the papers on "L'Atlantique" in *Dix-Huitième Siècle,* 33 (2001). The roundtable discussion at the American Historical Association meeting, Chicago, 2000, was entitled "The Atlantic World: Emerging Themes in a New Teaching Field." Cf. Nicholas P. Canny, "Writing Atlantic History; or, Reconfiguring the History of Colonial British America," *Journal of American History,* 86 (1999), 1093–1114; Canny, "Atlantic History: What and Why?" *European Review,* 9 (2001), 399–411; and David Armitage and Michael J. Braddick, eds., *The British Atlantic World, 1500–1800* (New York, 2002). The special issue of *Historical Reflections/ Réflexions Historiques,* 29 (2003), edited by Malick W. Ghachem, "Slavery and Citizenship in the Age of the Atlantic Revolutions," is a collection of papers from the Atlantic History Seminar.

2. *The New Republic,* Feb. 17, 1917, p. 60; Ronald Steel, *Walter Lippmann and the American Century* (Boston, 1980), p. 111; Thomas J. Knock, *To End All Wars: Woodrow Wilson and the Quest for a New World Order* (Princeton, N.J., 1992), pp. 119–120, 127, 201.

3. Forrest Davis, *The Atlantic System* (New York, 1941), p. xi.

4. Walter Lippmann, *U.S. War Aims* (Boston, 1944), pp. 78, 87; Steel, *Lippmann,* pp. 339, 380, 404ff.

5. Melvin Small, "The Atlantic Council—The Early Years" (MS) NATO report, June 1, 1998 (NATO website: www.nato.int/acad/fellow/96–98/small.pdf), pp. 9, 12, 14, 32, 34, 35; "The Atlantic Council," *The Atlantic Community Quarterly,* 1, no. 2 (1963) [preface]; "About this Quarterly," in ibid., no. 1 (1963), 4; ibid., nos. 3–4 (1963). I thank Kenneth Weisbrode for the reference to Small's useful paper and for other information about the Atlantic Council.

6. Ross Hoffman, "Europe and the Atlantic Community," *Thought,* 20 (1945), 25, 34. For his approach to the formulation of 1945, see his *The Great Republic* (New York, 1942), chap. vi. On Hoffman, see Patrick Allitt, *Catholic Intellectuals and Conservative Politics in America, 1950–1985* (Ithaca, N.Y., 1993), pp. 49–58. I wish to thank Professor John McGreevy for suggestions on the role of Catholic intellectuals in the public policy debates of this era and Professor Allitt for allowing me to see the manuscript of his book, *Catholic Converts: British and American Intellectuals Turn to Rome* (Ithaca, N.Y., 1997), which includes valuable information on Carlton Hayes.

7. Carlton J. H. Hayes, "The American Frontier—Frontier of What?" *American Historical Review,* 51 (1946), 206, 210, 208, 213 [hereafter *AHR*].

8. Frederick B. Tolles, *Quakers and the Atlantic Culture* (New York, 1960), pp. 3, x.

9. H. Hale Bellot, "Atlantic History," *History,* n.s., 31 (1946), 61–62.

10. Robert R. Palmer, "American Historians Remember Jacques Godechot," *French Historical Studies,* 61 (1990), 882; Jacques Godechot, *Histoire de l'Atlantique* ([Paris], 1947), pp. 1, 2, 332–333; C. N. Parkinson, *History,* n.s., 34 (1949), 260. Five years later Godechot was still thinking of the Atlantic in narrow terms, as the source of economic problems for French coastal towns that led to grievances and appeals for help from the national government on the eve of the Revolution. Godechot, "La France et les problèmes de l'Atlantique à la veille de la Révolution," *Revue du Nord,* 39, no. 142 (1954), 231–244.

11. Jacques Pirenne, *Grands Courants de l'Histoire Universelle* (Neuchâtel, 1944–1956), III; Michael Kraus, *The Atlantic Civilization: Eighteenth-Century Origins* ([1949] Ithaca, N.Y., 1966), pp. viii, 308–314; Vitorino Magalhães Godinho, "Problèmes d'économie atlantique: Le Portugal, les flottes du sucre et les flottes de l'or (1670–1770)," *Annales, économies, sociétés, civilisations,* 5 (1950), 184–197; Max Silberschmidt, "Wirtschaftshistorische Aspekte der Neueren Geschichte: Die Atlantische Gemeinschaft," *Historische Zeitschrift,* 171 (1951), 245–261; Huguette and Pierre Chaunu, "Économie atlantique. Économie mondiale (1504–1650): Problèmes de fait et de méthode," *Cahiers d'Histoire Mondiale—Journal of World History—Cuadernos de Historia Mundial,* 1 (1953), 91–104 (English translation in Peter Earle, ed., *Essays in European Economic History, 1500–1800* [Oxford, 1974], pp. 113–126); Huguette Chaunu and Pierre Chaunu, *Séville et l'Atlantique (1504–1650)*... (Paris, 1955–1959), I, ix.

12. Charles Verlinden, "Les Origines coloniales de la civilisation atlantique," *Cahiers d'Histoire Mondiale—Journal of World History—Cuadernos de Historia Mundial,* 1 (1953), 378, 398, 383.

13. UNESCO, Informatory Circular (CUA 52, June 29, 1953), and Basic Paper (CUA 57, February 9, 1954); Lucien Febvre et al., *Le Nouveau Monde et l'Europe*... (Neuchâtel, 1955).

14. Herbert Bolton, "The Epic of Greater America," *AHR,* 38 (1933), 448–474; Pedro Armillas, *The Native Period in the History of the New World,* trans. Glenda Crevenna and Theo Crevenna (Mexico City, 1962), vol. I of the series *Program of the History of America;* Silvio Zavala, *The Colonial Period in the History of the New World,* trans. Max Savelle (Mexico City, 1962), vol. II of *Program of the History of America,* pp. xii–xiii. Zavala's original, full-length work appeared after the translated, abridged version: *El Mundo Americano en la Epoca Colonial* (Mexico City, 1967), 2 vols.; Charles C. Griffin, *The National Period in the History of the New World: An Outline and Commentary* (Mexico City, 1961), vol. III of *Program of the History of America;* Roy F. Nichols, "A United States Historian's Appraisal of the History of America Project," *Revista de Historia de America,* 43 (1957), 144–158.

15. John Parry, "Critique," in *Programa de Historia de America: Introducciones y Comentarios* (Mexico City, 1955), pp. 66–73; Charles Verlinden, *The Beginnings of Modern Colonization . . . ,* trans. Yvonne Freccero (Ithaca, N.Y., 1970), pp. 74–75 (Spanish original in *Atlantida,* 4 [1966], 295–296); idem, *Les Origines de la Civilisation Atlantique: De la Renaissance à l'Age des Lumières* (Paris, 1966), pp. 7–8; Verlinden's view is referred to by Zavala in "A General View of the Colonial History of the New World," *AHR,* 66 (1961), 918; Zavala, *Colonial Period,* pp. xii–xiii, xxviii; Lewis Hanke, ed., *Do the Americas Have a Common History? A Critique of the Bolton Theory* (New York, 1964), p. 43; Charles Gibson, in *Handbook of Latin American Studies, No. 25* (Gainesville, Fla., 1963), p. 197. Cf. the symposium, "Have the Americas a Common History?" *Canadian Historical Review,* 23 (1942), 125–156.

16. Palmer, "Historians Remember Godechot," p. 882; Palmer, "The World Revolution of the West, 1763–1801," *Political*

Science Quarterly, 69 (1954), 4; Palmer, "Reflections on the French Revolution," *Political Science Quarterly,* 57 (1952), 66.

17. Jacques Godechot and Robert R. Palmer, "Le Problème de l'Atlantique du XVIIIème au XXème Siècle," *Relazioni del X Congresso Internazionale di Scienze Storiche* (Florence, [1955]), V *(Storia Contemporanea),* 175–177, 180, 202, 208, 207, 204, 216–219, 238.

18. Palmer, "Historians Remember Godechot," p. 883. The respondents cited: Donald McKay, G. S. Graham, Charles Webster, B. F. Hyslop, B. Lesnodorski, Eric Hobsbawm. *Atti del X Congresso Internazionale, Roma 4–11 Settembre 1955 . . .* (Rome, [1957]), pp. 566–579.

19. Palmer, "Historians Remember Godechot," p. 883.

20. Bernard Bailyn, "The Challenge of Modern Historiography," *AHR,* 87 (1982), 11–18.

21. Chaunu and Chaunu, *Séville et l'Atlantique,* VIII (part 1), 5, xiii, 7–8, 12–16; Manoel Cardozo, review, *AHR,* 68 (1963), 437–438; Roland Hussey, review, *AHR,* 63 (1958), 731.

22. Philip D. Curtin, *The Atlantic Slave Trade: A Census* (Madison, Wisc., 1969); idem, "Revolution and Decline in Jamaica, 1830–1865: The Role of Ideas in a Colonial Society" (Ph.D. diss., Harvard University, 1953); idem, *Two Jamaicas: The Role of Ideas in a Tropical Colony, 1830–1865* (Cambridge, Mass., 1955); idem, *The Image of Africa: British Ideas and Action, 1750–1850* (Madison, Wisc., 1964); idem, ed., *Africa Remembered: Narratives by West Africans from the Era of the Slave Trade* (Madison, Wisc., 1967); idem, *Economic Change in Precolonial Africa: Senegambia in the Era of the Slave Trade* (Madison, Wisc., 1975); Paul E. Lovejoy, *Africans in Bondage: . . . Essays in Honor of Philip D. Curtin . . .* (Madison, Wisc., 1986). Among the notable works along the way acknowledging Curtin were Herbert S. Klein, *The Middle Passage . . .* (Princeton, N.J., 1978); Henry A. Gemery and Jan

S. Hogendorn, eds., *The Uncommon Market: Essays in the Economic History of the Atlantic Slave Trade* (New York, 1979); and Barbara L. Solow, ed., *Slavery and the Rise of the Atlantic System* (Cambridge, 1991).

23. David Eltis, Stephen Behrendt, David Richardson, and Herbert S. Klein, eds., *The Trans-Atlantic Slave Trade: A Database on CD-ROM* (Cambridge, 1999); see the special issue devoted to the *Database: William and Mary Quarterly*, 3d ser., 58 (Jan. 2001) [hereafter *WMQ*].

24. Abbot E. Smith, "The Transportation of Convicts to the American Colonies in the Seventeenth Century," *AHR*, 39 (1934), 232–249; idem, *Colonists in Bondage: White Servitude and Convict Labor in America, 1607–1776* (Chapel Hill, N.C., 1947); Mildred Campbell, "Social Origins of Some Early Americans," in James M. Smith, ed., *Seventeenth-Century America: Essays in Colonial History* (Chapel Hill, N.C., 1959), pp. 63–89; David W. Galenson, *White Servitude in Colonial America: An Economic Analysis* (Cambridge, 1981); David W. Galenson, "'Middling People' or 'Common Sort'?: The Social Origins of Some Early Americans Reexamined," with a Rebuttal by Mildred Campbell, *WMQ*, 35 (1978), 499–540; David W. Galenson, "The Social Origins of Some Early Americans: Rejoinder," with a Reply by Mildred Campbell, *WMQ*, 36 (1979), 264–286; Bernard Bailyn, *Voyagers to the West . . .* (New York, 1986); A. Roger Ekirch, *Bound for America: The Transportation of British Convicts to the Colonies, 1718–1775* (Oxford, 1987). Later, Alison Games would make use of another London Port Register (1635) in her *Migration and the Origins of the English Atlantic World* (Cambridge, Mass., 1999).

25. Aubrey C. Land, Lois G. Carr, and Edward C. Papenfuse, eds., *Law, Society, and Politics in Early Maryland . . .* (Baltimore, 1977); Thad W. Tate and David L. Ammerman, eds., *The Chesapeake in the Seventeenth Century* (Chapel Hill,

N.C., 1979); Lois G. Carr, Philip D. Morgan, and Jean B. Russo, eds., *Colonial Chesapeake Society* (Chapel Hill, N.C., 1988). Among the important ancillary works are Russell R. Menard, "Population, Economy, and Society in Seventeenth-Century Maryland," *Maryland Historical Magazine,* 79 (1984), 71–92; Lois G. Carr, Russell R. Menard, and Lorena S. Walsh, *Robert Cole's World: Agriculture and Society in Early Maryland* (Chapel Hill, N.C., 1991); Lois G. Carr and Lorena S. Walsh, "The Planter's Wife: The Experiences of White Women in Seventeenth-Century Maryland," *WMQ,* 34 (1977), 542–571; Darrett B. Rutman and Anita H. Rutman, *A Place in Time: Middlesex County, Virginia, 1650–1750* (New York, 1984); James Horn, *Adapting to a New World: English Society in the Seventeenth-Century Chesapeake* (Chapel Hill, N.C., 1994).

26. Marianne S. Wokeck, "The Flow and the Composition of German Immigration to Philadelphia, 1727–1775," *Pennsylvania Magazine of History and Biography,* 105 (1981), 249–278; idem, *Trade in Strangers: The Beginnings of Mass Migration to North America* (University Park, Pa., 1999); Bernard Bailyn, *The Peopling of British North America: An Introduction* (New York, 1986), chap. i.

27. A. G. Roeber, *Palatines, Liberty, and Property: German Lutherans in Colonial British America* (Baltimore, 1993); Aaron S. Fogleman, *Hopeful Journeys: German Immigration, Settlement, and Political Culture in Colonial America* (Philadelphia, 1996); Bernard Bailyn and Philip D. Morgan, eds., *Strangers within the Realm: Cultural Margins of the First British Empire* (Chapel Hill, N.C., 1991), especially pp. 220ff.

28. Mack Walker, *The Salzburg Transaction: Expulsion and Redemption in Eighteenth-Century Germany* (Ithaca, N.Y., 1992), p. 140; George F. Jones, *The Salzburger Story* (Athens, Ga., 1984).

29. Bailyn and Morgan, eds., *Strangers within the Realm;* Kerby

Miller, *Emigrants and Exiles: Ireland and the Irish Exodus to North America* (New York, 1985); Nicholas Canny, ed., *Europeans on the Move: Studies on European Migration, 1500–1800* (Oxford, 1994); David H. Fischer, *Albion's Seed: Four British Folkways in America* (New York, 1989). Cf. Forum on *Albion's Seed* in *WMQ*, 48 (1991), 223–308.

30. Angel Rosenblat, *La población de America: desde 1492 hasta la actualidad* (Buenos Aires, 1945); John TePaske, "Spanish America: The Colonial Period," in Roberto Esquenazi-Mayo and Michael C. Meyer, eds., *Latin American Scholarship since World War II* . . . (Lincoln, Nebr., 1971), pp. 7–8; Julian H. Steward, review of Rosenblat, *La población de America* . . ., in *Hispanic American Historical Review,* 26 (1946), 353–356 [hereafter *HAHR*]; David P. Henige, *Numbers from Nowhere: The American Indian Contact Population Debate* (Norman, Okla., 1998), pp. 8–10; Sherburne F. Cook and Woodrow Borah, *Essays in Population History* . . . (Berkeley, Calif., 1971–1979): vols. I and II are subtitled *Mexico and the Caribbean,* vol. III *Mexico and California; Bibliography of Magnus Mörner, 1947–1990* (Stockholm, 1990); Magnus Mörner, *Race Mixture in the History of Latin America* (Boston, 1967); Woodrow Borah, "The Mixing of Populations," in Fredi Chiappelli, ed., *First Images of America: The Impact of the New World on the Old* (Berkeley, Calif., 1976), II, 707ff; David E. Stannard, *American Holocaust: Columbus, Christianity, and the Conquest of the Americas* (New York, 1992); Kirkpatrick Sale, *The Conquest of Paradise: Christopher Columbus and the Columbian Legacy* (New York, 1990).

31. James Lockhart, "The Social History of Latin America: Evolution and Potential," *Latin American Research Review,* 7 (1972), 17–18; Peter Boyd-Bowman, *Patterns of Spanish Emigration to the New World (1493–1580)* (Buffalo, N.Y., 1973); idem, "Spanish Emigrants to the Indies, 1595–98: A Profile,"

in Chiappelli, ed., *First Images of America,* II, 723–735; idem, "The Regional Origins of the Earliest Spanish Colonists of America," *Publications of the Modern Language Association of America,* 71 (1956), 1163n23.

32. Lockhart, "Social History of Latin America," pp. 13, 15–16, 8, 12, 32, 19–21, 27–30; Mark A. Burkholder and D. S. Chandler, *From Impotence to Authority* (Columbia, Mo., 1977); idem, *Biographical Dictionary of Audiencia Ministers in the Americas, 1687–1821* (Westport, Conn., 1982); Lockhart, *The Men of Cajamarca: A Social and Biographical Study of the First Conquerors of Peru* (Austin, 1972); David A. Brading, *Miners and Merchants in Bourbon Mexico, 1763–1810* (Cambridge, 1971).

33. Stanley J. Stein and Barbara H. Stein, *The Colonial Heritage of Latin America: Essays on Economic Dependence in Perspective* (New York, 1970), pp. 17, 21, 45, 47; P. J. Bakewell, *Silver Mining and Society in Colonial Mexico . . .* (Cambridge, 1971); Brading, *Miners and Merchants in Bourbon Mexico;* Lewis Hanke, *The Imperial City of Potosí* (The Hague, 1956), pp. 33–37.

34. Jacob M. Price, "The Tobacco Trade and the Treasury, 1685–1733: British Mercantilism in Its Fiscal Aspects" (Ph.D. diss., Harvard University, 1954); idem, *Tobacco in Atlantic Trade: The Chesapeake, London and Glasgow, 1675–1775* (Aldershot, Eng., 1995); idem, *The Atlantic Frontier of the Thirteen Colonies and States* (Aldershot, Eng., 1996); idem, *Overseas Trade and Traders: Essays on Some Commercial, Financial and Political Challenges Facing British Atlantic Merchants, 1660–1775* (Aldershot, Eng., 1996); idem, "The Tobacco Adventure to Russia . . . ," in *Transactions of the American Philosophical Society,* n.s., 51, part 1, (1961); idem, *France and the Chesapeake: A History of the French Tobacco Monopoly, 1674–1791, and of Its Relationship to the British and American Tobacco Trades* (Ann Arbor, Mich., 1973).

35. John G. Clark, *La Rochelle and the Atlantic Economy during the Eighteenth Century* (Baltimore, 1981); Paul G. Clemens, *The Atlantic Economy and Colonial Maryland's Eastern Shore: From Tobacco to Grain* (Ithaca, N.Y., 1980); David H. Sacks, *The Widening Gate: Bristol and the Atlantic Economy, 1450–1700* (Berkeley, Calif., 1991); Kenneth Morgan, *Bristol and the Atlantic Trade in the Eighteenth Century* (Cambridge, 1993); Franklin W. Knight and Peggy K. Liss, eds., *Atlantic Port Cities: Economy, Culture, and Society in the Atlantic World, 1650–1850* (Knoxville, Tenn., 1991); Bernard Bailyn, *The New England Merchants in the Seventeenth Century* (Cambridge, Mass., 1955), pp. 87–91; Frederick B. Tolles, *Meeting House and Counting House: The Quaker Merchants of Colonial Philadelphia, 1682–1763* ([1948] New York, 1963), pp. 89–95; Thomas M. Doerflinger, *A Vigorous Spirit of Enterprise: Merchants and Economic Development in Revolutionary Philadelphia* (Chapel Hill, N.C., 1986), p. 61.

36. Oliver A. Rink, *Holland on the Hudson: An Economic and Social History of Dutch New York* (Ithaca, N.Y., 1986), chap. vii.

37. Bernard Bailyn, *The Origins of American Politics* (New York, 1968), esp. pp. vii–ix.

38. Clarence H. Haring, *The Spanish Empire in America* (New York, 1947), pp. 127–129, 148, 345–347; Burkholder and Chandler, *Biographical Dictionary of Audiencia Ministers,* pp. xi–xxiii; idem, *From Impotence to Authority*; Mark A. Burkholder, ed., *Administrators of Empire* (Aldershot, Eng., 1998), essays 1, 2, 4, 8, 9, 12, 14, 16; James A. Henretta, *"Salutary Neglect": Colonial Administration under the Duke of Newcastle* (Princeton, N.J., 1972), pp. 220–221; Stanley N. Katz, *Newcastle's New York: Anglo-American Politics, 1732–1753* (Cambridge, Mass., 1968); Michael Kammen, *Empire and Interest* (Philadelphia, 1970); Alison G. Olson and Richard M. Brown, eds., *Anglo-American Political Relations,*

1675–1775 (New Brunswick, N.J., 1970); Alison G. Olson, *Anglo-American Politics, 1660–1775* (New York, 1973).

39. Stephen S. Webb, *The Governors-General: The English Army and the Definition of the Empire, 1569–1681* (Chapel Hill, N.C., 1979), p. xviii. Cf. Webb, *Lord Churchill's Coup: The Anglo-American Empire and the Glorious Revolution Reconsidered* (New York, 1995).

40. Alison G. Olson, *Making the Empire Work: London and American Interest Groups, 1690–1790* (Cambridge, Mass., 1991), p. xiii.

41. For a vivid example of the influence of European foreign relations on domestic affairs in America, see Patrice L. R. Higonnet, "The Origins of the Seven Years' War," *Journal of Modern History,* 40 (1968), 57–90. For the general loss of American influence on the eve of the Revolution, see Michael G. Kammen, *A Rope of Sand: The Colonial Agents, British Politics, and the American Revolution* (Ithaca, N.Y., 1968), chaps. x–xv. For an early example of ambitions frustrated, see Kenneth A. Lockridge, *The Diary, and Life, of William Byrd II of Virginia, 1674–1744* (Chapel Hill, N.C., 1987); for later examples, John A. Schutz, "Succession Politics in Massachusetts, 1730–1741," *WMQ,* 15 (1958), 508–520; Schutz, *William Shirley . . .* (Chapel Hill, N.C., 1961), esp. pp. 168ff.

42. Franco Venturi, *Utopia and Reform in the Enlightenment* (Cambridge, 1971), p. 130; Caroline Robbins, *The Eighteenth-Century Commonwealthman . . .* (Cambridge, Mass., 1959); Bernard Bailyn, *Ideological Origins of the American Revolution* (Cambridge, Mass., 1967); J. G. A. Pocock, "Machiavelli, Harrington, and English Political Ideologies in the Eighteenth Century," *WMQ,* 22 (1965), 549–583; idem, *The Machiavellian Moment: Florentine Political Thought and the Atlantic Republican Tradition* (Princeton, N.J., 1975).

43. Benjamin Keen, "Main Currents in United States Writing on

Colonial Spanish America, 1884–1984," *HAHR*, 65 (1985), 666–667.

44. D. W. Meinig, *The Shaping of America: A Geographical Perspective on 500 Years of History* (New Haven, Conn., 1986–1998), I *(Atlantic America, 1492–1800),* 64–65.

II. On the Contours of Atlantic History

1. David Eltis, "Atlantic History in Global Perspective," *Itinerario,* 23, no. 2 (1999), 141.

2. Horst Pietschmann, "Introduction: Atlantic History—History between European History and Global History," in Pietschmann, ed., *Atlantic History: History of the Atlantic System 1580–1830* . . . (Göttingen, 2002), pp. 35, 39, 40, 43; Renate Pieper, *Die Vermittlung einer neuen Welt: Amerika im Nachrichtennetz des Habsburgischen Imperiums, 1493–1598* (Mainz, 2000).

3. James Lockhart, "The Social History of Latin America: Evolution and Potential," *Latin American Research Review,* 7 (1972), 10, 14.

4. Cf. Fernand Braudel, *The Mediterranean and the Mediterranean World in the Age of Phillip II,* trans. Siân Reynolds ([1949] New York, 1972).

5. John H. Elliott, "Introduction: Colonial Identity in the Atlantic World," in Nicholas Canny and Anthony Pagden, eds., *Colonial Identity in the Atlantic World, 1500–1800* (Princeton, N.J., 1987), pp. 5–7.

6. John H. Elliott, "The Spanish Conquest and Settlement of America," in Leslie Bethell, ed., *The Cambridge History of Latin America* (Cambridge, 1984–), I, 162 [hereafter *CHLA*]. For the Spanish debate over the Indians' "barbarism" see José de Acosta, *De Procuranda Indorum Salute,* trans. and ed. G. Stewart McIntosh ([1588] Tayport, Scotland, [1996]), I, 4–6; John H. Elliott, *The Old World and*

the New, *1492–1650* (Cambridge, 1970), pp. 46–50; Anthony Pagden, *The Fall of Natural Man . . .* (Cambridge, 1982), pp. 123ff.

7. C. R. Friedrichs, "The War and German Society," in Geoffrey Parker, ed., *The Thirty Years' War* (New York, 1984), pp. 208–215; Geoffrey Parker, *Empire, War and Faith in Early Modern Europe* (London, 2002), pp. 150–168; Robert Ergang, *The Myth of the All-Destructive Fury of the Thirty Years' War* (Pocono Pines, Pa., 1956); Barbara Donagan, "Atrocity, War Crime, and Treason in the English Civil War," *AHR,* 99 (1994), 1137–1166.

8. Bartolomé de Las Casas, *The Devastation of the Indies: A Brief Account,* trans. Herma Briffault (New York, 1974), pp. 111, 43–44; Edward Waterhouse, *A Declaration of the State of the Colony and Affaires in Virginia . . .* (London, 1622), reprinted in Susan M. Kingsbury, ed., *The Records of the Virginia Company of London* (Washington, D.C., 1906–1935), III, 557; Treasurer and Council for Virginia to Gov. Francis Wyatt and the Governor's Council in Virginia, August 1, 1622, reprinted in Kingsbury, ed., *Records of Virginia Company,* III, 672; George Percy, "Trewe Relacyon . . . [1609–1612]," in *Tyler's Quarterly Historical and Genealogical Magazine,* 3 (1921–1922), 271–273. Richard Hakluyt's term for the "old soldiours trained up in the Netherlands" appears in the dedication of his translation of the Portuguese account of De Soto's expedition to Florida (1557)—a typical transcultural fusion—*Virginia Richly Valued . . .* (London, 1609), A4 verso.

9. Joyce Chaplin, *Subject Matter: Technology, the Body, and Science on the Anglo-American Frontier, 1500–1676* (Cambridge, Mass., 2001), pp. 264–265, 268–270. ("The worst instances of Anglo-Indian warfare in fact showed that the English had much in common with Spaniards." p. 178)

10. Allen W. Trelease, *Indian Affairs in Colonial New York:*

The Seventeenth Century (Ithaca, N.Y., 1960), p. 72; E. B. O'Callaghan, *History of New Netherland . . .* (New York, 1848), I, 269.

11. Richard S. Dunn, *Sugar and Slaves: The Rise of the Planter Class in the English West Indies, 1624–1713* (Chapel Hill, N.C., 1972), p. 320.

12. William Bradford, *Of Plymouth Plantation, 1620–1649,* ed. Samuel E. Morison (New York, 1952), p. 296; Charles Orr, *History of the Pequot War: The Contemporary Accounts of Mason, Underhill, Vincent and Gardener* (Cleveland, 1897), p. 81.

13. Fynes Moryson, *An Itinerary . . . containing His Ten Yeeres Travell . . .* ([1617] Glasgow, 1907–1908), IV, 185; Nicholas P. Canny, *The Elizabethan Conquest of Ireland: A Pattern Established, 1565–76* (New York, 1976), pp. 160–161, 33–34, 66–67, 126–127; idem, "Atlantic History: What and Why?" *European Review,* 9 (2001), 406; David B. Quinn, *England and the Discovery of America, 1481–1620 . . .* (London, 1974), pp. 286–287, chaps. x and iii; John Parker, *Books to Build an Empire: A Bibliographic History of English Overseas Interests to 1620* (Amsterdam, 1965), pp. 44–48, 77–81; David B. Quinn, "A List of Books Purchased for the Virginia Company," *Virginia Magazine of History and Biography,* 77 (1969), 347–360; idem, *England and the Discovery of America,* pp. 216–222; Jorge Cañizares-Esguerra, *Toward a Panamerican Atlantic: Nature, Narratives, and Identities,* chap. ii (". . . Atlanticizing Demonology"), forthcoming. I thank Professor Cañizares-Esguerra for allowing me to read and cite this chapter before its publication.

14. Waterhouse, *Declaration,* p. 561.

15. Canny, *Elizabethan Conquest,* pp. 127, 122; Vincent P. Carey, "John Derricke's *Image of Ireland,* Sir Henry Sidney, and the Massacre at Mullaghmast, 1578," *Irish Historical Studies,* 31 (1999), 309, 325.

16. Robert Bennett to Edward Bennett, June 9, 1623, in Kingsbury, ed., *Records of Virginia Company,* IV, 221–222.

17. Lewis Hanke, *The Spanish Struggle for Justice in the Conquest of America* (Philadelphia, 1949); idem, *All Mankind Is One . . .* (DeKalb, Ill., 1974); John H. Elliott, "Spain and America in the Sixteenth and Seventeenth Centuries," *CHLA,* I, 306–309; on Acosta, Jorge Cañizares-Esguerra, *How to Write the History of the New World: Histories, Epistemologies, and Identities in the Eighteenth-Century Atlantic World* (Stanford, Calif., 2001), esp. pp. 70–75, 82–83; on Vieira, Thomas M. Cohen, *The Fire of Tongues: António Vieira and the Missionary Church in Brazil and Portugal* (Stanford, Calif., 1998), and Charles R. Boxer, *A Great Luso-Brazilian Figure, Padre António Vieira, S. J., 1608–1697* (London, 1957); on Harriot, John W. Shirley, *Thomas Harriot: A Biography* (Oxford, 1983), pp. 151ff.

18. James A. Williamson, *English Colonies in Guiana and on the Amazon: 1604–1668* (Oxford, 1923), chap. iv and p. 186; Victor Enthoven, "A Dutch Crossing: Migration between the Netherlands, Africa, and the Americas, 1600–1800" (Working Paper, International Seminar on the History of the Atlantic World, 1500–1800, Harvard University, 2004), pp. 4, 8 [hereafter: Working Paper, Atlantic History Seminar]; Cornelius Goslinga, *The Dutch in the Caribbean and on the Wild Coast, 1580–1680* (Assen, The Netherlands, 1971), p. 433; O'Callaghan, *History of New Netherland,* II, 464–465.

19. The first colonists in the West Indies, Richard Pares wrote, were what he called "tough guys" of many European nations, who quarrelled, drank enormously, duelled, kidnapped, murdered, and rebelled against whatever authority they happened to fall under. Pares, *Merchants and Planters* (Cambridge, 1960: Supplement 4 of the *Economic History Review*), p. 15.

20. Dunn, *Sugar and Slaves,* pp. 256–258.

21. Ibid., p. 120; C. C. Hall, ed., *Narratives of Early Maryland,*

1633–1684 ([1910] New York, 1925), p. 34; Hilary McD. Beckles, "A 'riotous and unruly lot': Irish Indentured Servants and Freeman in the English West Indies, 1644–1713," *WMQ*, 47 (1990), 510, 518–520.

22. Kittiya Lee, "Among the Vulgar, the Erudite, and the Sacred: The Oral Life of Colonial Amazonia" (Working Paper, Atlantic History Seminar, 2004), pp. 1, 10; Dunn, *Sugar and Slaves,* p. 149.

23. Murdo J. Macleod, "Spain and America: The Atlantic Trade, 1492–1720," *CHLA,* I, 352–353; Donna Merwick, *Possessing Albany, 1630–1710: The Dutch and English Experiences* (Cambridge, 1990), esp. pp. 77–84.

24. Philip D. Morgan, *Slave Counterpoint. . .* (Chapel Hill, N.C., 1998), pp. 118, 534, 549, 581, 603, 622; Joseph S. Wood, *The New England Village* (Baltimore, 1997), chap. i, esp. pp. 37ff; Mark A. Burkholder and Lyman L. Johnson, *Colonial Latin America* (New York, 1990), pp. 174–182; James Horn, *Adapting to a New World: English Society in the Seventeenth-Century Chesapeake* (Chapel Hill, N.C., 1994), pp. 429, 427, 419; Lockhart, "Social History of Colonial Spanish America," p. 35.

25. Ida Altman, *Transatlantic Ties in the Spanish Empire: Brihuega, Spain, and Puebla, Mexico, 1560–1620* (Stanford, Calif., 2000), pp. 186, 185, 33, 37.

26. Dunn, *Sugar and Slaves,* pp. 281–286.

27. John H. Elliott, "Renaissance Europe and America: A Blunted Impact?" in Fredi Chiappelli, ed., *First Images of America: The Impact of the New World on the Old* (Berkeley, Calif., 1976), I, 20–21.

28. Elliott, *Old World and the New,* chaps. i, ii (quotation at p. 18; cf. p. 39); Henry R. Wagner and Helen R. Parish, *The Life and Writings of Bartolomé de Las Casas* (Albuquerque, 1967), p. 267; Benjamin Schmidt, "American Allies: The Dutch Encounter with the New World, 1492–1650" (Working Paper, Atlantic History Seminar, 1998), p. 4. For a full development

of this theme, see Schmidt, *Innocence Abroad: The Dutch Imagination and the New World, 1570–1670* (Cambridge, 2001). For the republications of José de Acosta's *Natural and Moral History of the Indies* (1590) and its translation "into all the principal languages of Europe," see David A. Brading, *The First America: The Spanish Monarchy, Creole Patriots, and the Liberal State, 1492–1867* (Cambridge, 1991), p. 184.

29. Shirley, *Thomas Harriot,* pp. 143ff. On graphic portrayals: Hugh Honour, *The New Golden Land: European Images of America from the Discoveries to the Present Time* (New York, 1975), chaps. i-iv; and Paul Hulton, ed., *America, 1585: The Complete Drawings of John White* (Chapel Hill, N.C., 1984).

30. Josep M. Barnadas, "The Catholic Church in Colonial Spanish America," *CHLA,* I, 515; Elliott, *Old World and the New,* pp. 25–27.

31. Anthony Pagden, *The Uncertainties of Empire . . .* (Aldershot, Eng., 1994), chap. v; *Utopia* may not have been only a source of Latin American idealism in the treatment of the Indians; it may also have been in part the product of it, if, as claimed, "both Plato and the New World discoveries played their part in the initial ideal of Utopia" and if Las Casas's *Memorial of Remedies for the Indies* (1516) helped shape More's thought in writing the book. Dominic Baker-Smith, "Utopia and the Franciscans," in A. D. Cousins and Damian Grace, eds., *More's Utopia and the Utopian Inheritance* (Lanham, Md., 1995), p. 50; Victor N. Baptiste, *Bartolomé de Las Casas and Thomas More's Utopia: Connections and Similarities . . .* (Culver City, Calif., 1990).

32. Elliott, "Spain and America," p. 307; Ida Altman, Sarah Cline, and Juan Javier Pescador, *The Early History of Greater Mexico* (Upper Saddlebrook, N.J., 2002), p. 125. On Quiroga, see Fintan B. Warren, *Vasco de Quiroga and His Pueblo-Hospitals of Santa Fe* (Washington, D.C., 1963), esp. chaps. iii, iv, vi, and ix, and Pagden, *Uncertainties of Empire,* chap. v; Silvio Zavala, "The American Utopia of the Sixteenth Century,"

Huntington Library Quarterly, 10 (1947), 337–347; Georges Baudot, *Utopia and History in Mexico . . . ,* trans. Bernard R. Ortiz de Montellano and Thelma Ortiz de Montellano ([1977] Niwot, Colo., 1995), pp. xv, 87, 88, 312, 92, 89, 245, 313, 398; John L. Phelan, *The Millennial Kingdom of the Franciscans in the New World . . .* (Berkeley, Calif., 1956); Ernest L. Tuveson, *Millennium and Utopia: A Study in the Background of the Idea of Progress* (Gloucester, Mass., 1972). On the Jesuits' "reductions," Barbara Ganson, *The Guaraní under Spanish Rule in the Río de la Plata* (Stanford, Calif., 2003); Philip Caraman, *The Lost Paradise: An Account of the Jesuits in Paraguay, 1607–1768* (London, 1975). On Motolinía, see Jacques Lafaye, *Quetzalcóatl and Guadalupe: The Formation of Mexican National Consciousness, 1531–1815,* trans. Benjamin Keen (Chicago, 1976), pp. 139–142.

33. J. F. Maclear, "New England and the Fifth Monarchy: The Quest for the Millennium in Early American Puritanism," *WMQ,* 32 (1975), 223–260 (quotations at pp. 223, 236); Richard W. Cogley, *John Eliot's Mission to the Indians before King Philip's War* (Cambridge, Mass., 1999), pp. 76–79, 114–115.

34. E. B. O'Callaghan et al., eds., *Documents Relative to the Colonial History of the State of New-York* (Albany, N.Y., 1856–1887), III, 346; on Plockhoy, see Leland Harder, "Plockhoy and His Settlement at Zwaanendael, 1663," *Mennonite Quarterly Review,* 23 (1949), 188; Leland Harder and Marvin Harder, *Plockhoy From Zurik-zee* (Newton, Kans., 1952), pp. 81–83, 16–17; Ellis L. Raesly, *Portrait of New Netherland* (New York, 1945), p. 290.

35. Bernard Bailyn, *The Peopling of British North America: An Introduction* (New York, 1986), pp. 123–124.

36. Christine Daniels and Michael V. Kennedy, eds., *Negotiated Empires . . . 1500–1820* (New York, 2002); Lee, "Among the Vulgar," p. 20; Dunn, *Sugar and Slaves,* pp. 165, 149, 151; Peggy Liss, *Atlantic Empires: The Network of Trade and Revolution, 1713–1826* (Baltimore, 1983), chap. iv; James

Lockhart and Stuart B. Schwartz, *Early Latin America* (Cambridge, 1983), p. 66; Burkholder and Johnson, *Colonial Latin America,* pp. 174–182; Womack, in personal correspondence.

37. Pietschmann, "Introduction: Atlantic History," pp. 14, 41.

38. John Thornton, *Africa and Africans in the Making of the Atlantic World, 1400–1680* ([1992] Cambridge, 1998), pp. 14–21, 41–42; D. W. Meinig, *The Shaping of America: A Geographical Perspective on 500 Years of History* (New Haven, Conn., 1986–1998), I *(Atlantic America, 1492–1800),* 6; Paul Butel, *The Atlantic,* trans. Iain H. Grant (New York, 1999), p. 3; Pierre and Huguette Chaunu, *Séville et l'Amérique aux XVIe et XVIIe siècles* (Paris, 1977), pp. 222, 224–225; Jacques Godechot and Robert R. Palmer, "Le Problème de l'Atlantique du XVIIIème au XXème Siècle," *Relazioni del X Congresso Internazionale di Scienze Storiche* (Florence, [1955]), V *(Storia Contemporanea),* 181–188.

39. Bernard Bailyn, *The New England Merchants in the Seventeenth Century* (Cambridge, Mass., 1955), pp. 82–85, 88; Larry Gragg, *Englishmen Transplanted: The English Colonization of Barbados, 1627–1660* (Oxford, 2003), pp. 109–110, 138–139.

40. Peter Coclanis, *The Shadow of a Dream: Economic Life and Death in the South Carolina Low Country, 1670–1920* (New York, 1989), p. 133; John J. McCusker and Russell Menard, *The Economy of British America, 1607–1789* (Chapel Hill, N.C., 1991), pp. 174–179. Table 8.2 shows 17 percent going to Southern Europe and 18 percent to the West Indies.

41. Butel, *Atlantic,* pp. 139–140; Paul Butel, "France, the Antilles, and Europe in the Seventeenth and Eighteenth Centuries: Renewal of Foreign Trade," in James D. Tracy, ed., *The Rise of Merchant Empires: Long-Distance Trade in the Early Modern World, 1350–1750* (Cambridge, 1990), p. 159; H. E. S. Fisher, *The Portugal Trade . . .* (London, 1971), esp. pp. 128–129, 138–139; Liss, *Atlantic Empires,* p. 83.

42. David Hancock, *Citizens of the World: London Merchants*

and the Integration of the British Atlantic Community, 1735–1785 (Cambridge, 1995); D. A. Farnie, "The Commercial Empire of the Atlantic, 1607–1783," *Economic History Review*, 2d ser., 15 (1962–1963), 205–218.

43. For another exhaustive study of the pan-Atlantic connections of major London firms—in this case Lascelles & Maxwell—see Simon D. Smith, "Merchants and Planters *Revisited*," *Economic History Review*, 2d ser., 55 (2002), 434–465, and idem, "Gedney Clarke of Salem and Barbados's Transatlantic Super-Merchant," *New England Quarterly*, 76 (2003), 499–549. On Bristol and the British-Portuguese connections: Kenneth Morgan, *Bristol and the Atlantic Trade in the Eighteenth Century* (Cambridge, 1993), pp. 9–10; Kenneth Maxwell, "The Atlantic in the Eighteenth Century: A Southern Perspective on the Need to Return to the 'Big Picture,'" *Transactions of the Royal Society*, 6th ser., 3 (1993), 219–220.

44. Butel, *Atlantic*, pp. 142, 154. Data on the Atlantic wine trade were generously supplied in correspondence by David Hancock from his forthcoming book on that subject. Enthoven, "Dutch Crossing," pp. 24, 27 estimates that of the 1.9 million people who left the Netherlands for Atlantic destinations, 700,000 remained abroad or died in transit, in contrast to the estimated 1 million who left for Asia, of whom approximately 630,000 did not return. On the relative importance of the Atlantic area and Asia for the Dutch, see the different views of Pieter Emmer and Wim Klooster, "The Dutch Atlantic, 1600–1900: Expansion without Empire," *Itinerario*, 23, no. 2 (1999), 48–66. For a broad coverage of the Dutch Atlantic, see Johannes Postma and Victor Enthoven, eds., *Riches from Atlantic Commerce: Dutch Transatlantic Trade and Shipping, 1585–1817* (Leiden, 2003).

   On the Atlantic trading contacts of the Sephardic Jews, see Paolo Bernedini and Norman Fiering, eds., *The Jews and the Expansion of Europe to the West, 1450–1800* (New York,

2001), chaps. xiv (Jews in French trade: Bordeaux), xviii (in Surinam and Curaçao; population figures, p. 353), xxi (in the slave trade), xxii (in Portuguese and Atlantic commerce), and xxiv (as mediators and innovators in Europe's westward expansion). Cf. map 11, p. 449. See also Enthoven, "Dutch Crossing," pp. 18–21 and citations there; and Wim Klooster, "Curaçao and the Caribbean Transit Trade," in Postma and Enthoven, eds., *Riches from Atlantic Commerce*, p. 205.

On Curaçao's and St. Eustatius's penetration of mercantilist barriers: Linda Rupert, "'Sailing Suspicious Routes': . . . Inter-Imperial Trade between Curaçao and Venezuela" (Working Paper, Atlantic History Seminar, 2004); Wim Klooster, *Illicit Riches: Dutch Trade in the Caribbean* (Leiden, 1998) and idem, "Curaçao and the Caribbean Transit Trade."

45. "The first full-blown mercantilism in the Spanish Empire," Carla Phillips writes, "appeared only with the Bourbon reforms of the eighteenth century." Phillips, "The Growth and Composition of Trade in the Iberian Empires, 1450–1750," in Tracy, ed., *Rise of Merchant Empires*, p. 96; Butel, *Atlantic*, p. 128; "France was the chief supplier of manufactured goods for Spain and, via Cádiz, for its American empire . . . It was always America that guided French commercial growth, from mid [eighteenth] century to the eve of the American Revolution." Butel, "Renewal of Foreign Trade," pp. 162, 170; Stanley J. Stein and Barbara H. Stein, *Silver, Trade, and War: Spain and America in the Making of Early Modern Europe* (Baltimore, 2000), pp. 81, 86, 265, 71, 72; Liss, *Atlantic Empires*, p. 50.

46. Wim Klooster, "An Overview of Dutch Trade with the Americas, 1600–1800," in Postma and Enthoven, eds., *Riches from Atlantic Commerce*, p. 378; Stein and Stein, *Silver, Trade, and War*, pp. 18, 88, 25, 264. Spain's protectionism in the sixteenth century, "bullionist in intent, in practice episodic and ineffec-

tive," undermined its production of goods, which were increasingly supplied by Spain's northern neighbors. "Consequently the great surge of colonial precious metals exports between 1580 and 1630 and corresponding colonial demand for imports increasingly bypassed the metropolitan economy, stimulating instead Genoese, Flemish, Dutch, English, and French artisans, merchants, and shippers," pp. 86–87. Cf. McCusker and Menard, *Economy of British America,* pp. 77–78 and especially n10. Earl J. Hamilton estimated that 10–50 percent of the gold and silver imported into Spain never appeared in the official registers; Phillips, "Trade in the Iberian Empires," p. 85n107; on fluctuations in smuggling of gold to Spain, ibid., p. 94.

47. A. J. R. Russell-Wood, "Colonial Brazil: The Gold Cycle, c. 1690–1750," *CHLA,* II, 589ff, esp. pp. 591–593; on the Brazilian gold boom in the eighteenth century, see Phillips, "Trade in the Iberian Empires," p. 65.

48. McCusker and Menard, *Economy of British America,* p. 78; Stein and Stein, *Silver, Trade, and War,* pp. 79, 85, 84, 69; Lawrence H. Gipson, *The Coming of the Revolution, 1763–1775* (New York, 1954), chap. iii, pp. 60–64; idem, "The American Revolution," *Canadian Historical Review,* 23 (1942), 38. Twenty years later Gipson reduced his estimate of the distilleries' needs to 20,000. *The British Empire before the American Revolution* (Caldwell, Id., 1936–1970), X, 113–114.

Butel, *Atlantic,* pp. 164, 104, 126, 147. France supplied more than 87 percent of North America's imported molasses. One-half of all Caribbean imports to North America may have come from the French islands, and New England handled much of that trade. On that estimate, and on the negative balance of New England's import trade with Britain in the eighteenth century and the region's hugely profitable export trade to the Caribbean—the illicit trade with the French islands providing "a key factor in promoting New England's prosperity after 1750"—see David Richardson, "Slavery, Trade, and Economic Growth in Eighteenth Century New England," in Barbara L. Solow, ed., *Slavery and the Rise of the Atlantic System* (Cambridge, 1991), pp. 248–262 and Richard Pares, *Yankees and Creoles: The Trade between North America and the West Indies before the American Revolution* (Cambridge, Mass., 1956).

49. Butel, *Atlantic*, pp. 108, 150, 159; J. H. Parry, "Transport and Trade Routes," in J. H. Clapham et al., eds., *The Cambridge Economic History of Europe* (Cambridge, 1941–1989), IV, 201–202; Stein and Stein, *Silver, Trade, and War*, pp. 191, 107, 109–116; Liss, *Atlantic Empires*, p. 75; Allan Christelow, "Contraband Trade between Jamaica and the Spanish Main . . . ," *HAHR*, 22 (1942), 309–343; Klooster, *Illicit Riches*, pp. 1, 87.

50. Stein and Stein, *Silver, Trade, and War*, pp. 136–141, 264.

51. David Eltis, "The Volume and Structure of the Transatlantic Slave Trade: A Reassessment," *WMQ*, 58 (2001), 43, Table I. For the eighteenth century, in addition to Britain's share of the slave trade, Portugal carried 31 percent of the century's diaspora and France 18 percent.

52. Stephen D. Behrendt, "Markets, Transaction Cycles, and Profits: Merchant Decision Making in the British Slave Trade," *WMQ*, 58 (2001), 171–204.

53. P. J. Marshall, "The British in Asia: Trade to Dominion," in William R. Louis et al., eds., *Oxford History of the British Empire* (Oxford, 1998–1999), II, 489 and Marshall, "The English in Asia to 1700," I, chap. xii; Phillips, "Trade in the Iberian Empires," pp. 48–55; Thornton, *Africa and Africans*, p. 36; Butel, *Atlantic*, p. 103. Enthoven points out that the Dutch East India Company never wanted to create overseas settlements in Asia as the West India Company did in the Americas: "Dutch Crossing," p. 37.

54. English migration figures from Henry Gemery, "Emigration

from the British Isles to the New World, 1630–1700 . . . ," *Research in Economic History,* 5 (1980), 215, Table A.5; Spanish figures from Nicolas Sanchez-Albornoz, "The First Transatlantic Transfer: Spanish Migration to the New World, 1493–1810," in Nicholas Canny, ed., *Europeans on the Move: Studies on European Migration, 1500–1800* (Oxford, 1994), pp. 26–36; French figures from Leslie Choquette, *Frenchman into Peasants . . .* (Cambridge, Mass., 1997), pp. 20–22, 198, 303, chap. i; Leslie Choquette, "Frenchmen into Peasants: Modernity and Tradition in the Peopling of French North America," *Proceedings of the American Antiquarian Society,* 104 (1994), 32. On the composition of the Spanish migration, Ida Altman and James Horn, eds., *"To Make America": European Emigration in the Early Modern Period* (Berkeley, Calif., 1991), chaps. ii, iii.

55. Eltis, "Volume and Structure of the Slave Trade," Tables I, II, III; David B. Davis, *The Problem of Slavery in Western Culture* (Ithaca, N.Y., 1966), 248ff; Solow, ed., *Slavery,* p. 1.

56. Juan Javier Pescador, *The New World inside a Basque Village: The Oiartzun Valley and Its Atlantic Emigrants, 1550–1800* (Reno, Nev., 2004), p. 126; Liss, *Atlantic Empires,* pp. 52, 76.

57. Butel, *Atlantic,* p. 171; A. G. Roeber, *Palatines, Liberty, and Property: German Lutherans in Colonial British America* (Baltimore, 1993), p. 9, chap. iv; Aaron S. Fogleman, *Hopeful Journeys: German Immigration, Settlement, and Political Culture in Colonial America, 1717–1775* (Philadelphia, 1996), part I; Bailyn, *Peopling of British North America;* Alan L. Karres, *Sojourners in the Sun: Scottish Migrants in Jamaica and the Chesapeake, 1740–1800* (Ithaca, N.Y., 1992).

58. Francis J. Bremer, "Increase Mather's Friends: The Trans-Atlantic Congregational Network of the Seventeenth Century," *Proceedings of the American Antiquarian Society,* 94 (1984), 59–96; Bailyn, *New England Merchants,* p. 88.

59. Frank Klingberg, ed., *Codrington Chronicle: An Experiment*

in Anglican Altruism . . . (Berkeley, Calif., 1949), p. 7; Frederick B. Tolles, *Quakers and the Atlantic Culture* (New York, 1960), pp. 13, 23, 24, 26, 29; Rebecca Larson, *Daughters of Light: Quaker Women Preaching and Prophesying in the Colonies and Abroad, 1700–1775* (New York, 1999), app. 1, 2.

60. J. Taylor Hamilton, *A History of the Missions of the Moravian Church . . .* (Bethlehem, Pa., 1901), p. 209.

61. J. Taylor Hamilton and Kenneth G. Hamilton, *History of the Moravian Church . . .* ([1900] Bethlehem, Pa., 1967), chaps. iv, ix–xi, xiii.

62. Sydney E. Ahlstrom, *A Religious History of the American People* (New Haven, Conn., 1972), p. 243; Gillian L. Gollin, *Moravians in Two Worlds . . .* (New York, 1967), pp. 46–47.

63. Carola Wessel, "Connecting Congregations: The Net of Communications among the Moravians . . . (1772–1774)," in Craig D. Atwood and Peter Vogt, eds., *The Distinctiveness of Moravian Culture . . .* (Nazareth, Pa., 2003), p. 156.

64. Renate Wilson, "Continental Protestant Refugees and Their Protectors in Germany and London: Commercial and Charitable Networks," *Pietismus und Neuzeit*, 20 (1994), 108. Halle was the subject of a workshop at the Atlantic History Seminar, "The Halle Archives and the Pietist Diaspora," November 15–16, 1997. For the participants and program, see the Seminar website, www.fas.harvard.edu/~atlantic/hallewsp.html. The voluminous reports the missionaries sent back to Halle and copies of the materials they carried to their missions remain to this day on the shelves of the Foundations' archives: Thomas J. Müller-Bahlke and Jürgen Gröschl, eds., *Salzburg, Halle, Nordamerika* (Halle, 1999). For a full account, see Renate Wilson, *Pious Traders in Medicine: German Pharmaceutical Networks in Eighteenth-Century North America* (University Park, Pa., 2000). On the Jesuits: James Axtell, *The Invasion Within: The Contest of Cultures in Colonial North America* (New York, 1985), p. 276.

65. See Jacques Lafaye, "Literature and Intellectual Life in Colonial Spanish America," *CHLA,* II, 695. Cf. Lafaye, *Quetzalcóatl and Guadalupe,* p. 68.

66. Liss, *Atlantic Empires,* p. 85; Elliott, "Spain and America," pp. 314–319, 336; David A. Brading, "Bourbon Spain and its American Empire," *CHLA,* I, 402, 438–439.

67. John T. Lanning, *The Eighteenth-Century Enlightenment in the University of San Carlos de Guatemala* (Ithaca, N.Y., 1956), pp. 342–350; Lafaye, "Literature and Intellectual Life," pp. 675–676, 696.

68. Jaime E. Rodríguez, *The Independence of Latin America* ([1996] Cambridge, 1998), pp. 13–19; Anthony Pagden and Nicholas Canny, "Afterword: From Identity to Independence," in Canny and Pagden, eds., *Colonial Identity in the Atlantic World,* pp. 270–272, 277; Brading, *First America,* pp. 450–462; Lafaye, "Intellectual Life in Spanish America," pp. 694–704; Paz, in Lafaye, *Quetzalcóatl and Guadalupe,* p. xvi; Jordana Dym, "Conceiving Central America: Public, Patria and Nation in the *Gazetta de Guatemala* (1797–1807)" (paper presented at New York University Graduate History Students Workshop, 1997), pp. 6, 8, 17. On the effect of the Bourbon reforms on the creole elite, see John Lynch, ed., *Latin American Revolutions, 1808–1826* (Norman, Okla., 1994), pp. 12–17, 27; on the creoles' incipient nationalism, pp. 34–37, 383–384.

69. Lafaye, *Quetzalcóatl and Guadalupe,* pp. xvi, xvii, chap. xv; Enrique Florescano, *Memory, Myth, and Time in Mexico: From the Aztecs to Independence,* trans. Albert G. Bork (Austin, 1994), chap. v ("Creole Patriotism, Independence, and the Appearance of a National History"); David A. Brading, *Mexican Phoenix: Our Lady of Guadalupe: Image and Tradition, 1531–2000* (New York, 2001), pp. 127–128, chap. viii; idem, *Prophecy and Myth in Mexican History* (Cambridge, 1984), pp. 28–31, 40; idem, *Classical Republicanism and Creole Pa-*

triotism: Simón Bolívar (1783–1830) and the Spanish American Revolution (Cambridge, 1983), pp. 7–8; Rodríguez, *Independence,* p. 1.

70. Richard Herr, *The Eighteenth-Century Revolution in Spain* (Princeton, N.J., 1958), chaps. ii, vi, p. 165; Liss, *Atlantic Empires,* pp. 92, 230; Charles E. Ronan, *Francisco Javier Clavigero, S. J. (1731–1787): Figure of the Mexican Enlightenment, His Life and Works* (Chicago, 1977), pp. 14–28, 20–23, 344–345; Brading, *First America,* chap. xx; idem, *Mexican Phoenix,* pp. 186–188; Anthony Pagden, *Spanish Imperialism and the Political Imagination: Studies in European and Spanish-American Social and Political Theory, 1513–1830* (New Haven, Conn., 1990), chap. iv; Florescano, *Memory, Myth, and Time in Mexico,* chap. v; Benjamin Keen, *The Aztec Image in Western Thought* (New Brunswick, N.J., 1971), pp. 292–300.

    On John Trenchard and Thomas Gordon as major publicists of reformist ideals: Bernard Bailyn, *Ideological Origins of the American Revolution,* (enl. ed., Cambridge, Mass., 1992), pp. 35–36, 43–45 and specific citations throughout. On the slow extrication of Enlightenment thought from traditional scholasticism in the Spanish American universities see John T. Lanning, *Academic Culture in the Spanish Colonies* (Port Washington, N.Y., 1940), esp. chap. iii; Arthur P. Whitaker, ed., *Latin America and the Enlightenment* (Ithaca, N.Y., 1961), esp. essays by Lanning and Griffin; and Rodríguez, *Independence,* chap. ii.

71. John L. Phelan, *The People and the King: The Comunero Revolution in Colombia, 1781* (Madison, Wisc., 1978), p. xviii.

72. Emma Rothschild, "David Hume and the Sea-Gods of the Atlantic" (Working Paper, Centre for History and Economics, King's College, Cambridge, 2004), pp. 39, 48. Quoted with the kind permission of the author.

73. Mark G. Spencer, ed., *Hume's Reception in Early America* (2 vols.; Bristol, Eng., 2002); Bernard Bailyn, *To Begin the*

World Anew: The Genius and Ambiguities of the American Founders (New York, 2003), chap. v; Brading, *First America*, pp. 608–620; idem, *Classical Republicanism and Creole Patriotism.*

74. Franco Venturi, *Utopia and Reform in the Enlightenment* (Cambridge, 1971), chap. iv; Michel Porret, ed., *Beccaria et la culture juridique des Lumières* . . . (Geneva, 1997); William W. Pierson, Jr., "Foreign Influences on Venezuelan Political Thought, 1830–1930," *HAHR*, 15 (1935), 8–9; Jonathan Harris, "Berandino Rivadavia and Benthamite 'Discipleship,'" *Latin American Research Review*, 33 (1998), 129–149; Beatriz Dávilo, "Travels, Correspondence, and Newspapers in the Constitution of Transatlantic Political and Intellectual Networks, Río de la Plata, 1810–1825" (Working Paper, Atlantic History Seminar, 2003); Ruth Pike, "Penal Servitude in the Spanish Empire: Presidio Labor in the Eighteenth Century," *HAHR*, 58 (1978); H. L. A. Hart, *Essays on Bentham: Studies in Jurisprudence and Political Theory* (Oxford, 1982), chap. ii and pp. 40–52. In the documentary appendixes to his edition of *Dei Delitti E Delle Pene* . . . (Turin, 1978), Venturi traces Beccaria's influence in Italy, France, England, Spain, Switzerland, Austria, Germany, Denmark, Sweden, and Russia. On the banning of Bentham's treatises: David Bushnell, ed., Frederick H. Fornoff, trans., *El Libertador: Writings of Simón Bolívar* (New York, 2003), pp. 214–215.

75. Arthur Sheps, "The American Revolution and the Transformation of English Republicanism," *Historical Reflections/ Réflexions Historiques*, 10 (1975), 3, 6, 26–28; Bailyn, *To Begin the World Anew*, chap. v.

76. Godechot and Palmer, "Le Problème de l'Atlantique," pp. 204, 226; Lynch, ed., *Latin American Revolutions*, p. 33; Rodríguez, *Independence*, p. 246.

77. Bolívar to Juan José Flores, Nov. 9, 1830; "The Angostura Address," Feb. 15, 1819, in Bushnell, ed., *El Libertador*, pp. 146, 36, 53. Cf. Brading, *Prophecy and Myth*, p. 51.

Acknowledgments

I AM grateful to John Womack for his critique of an early draft of these papers which kept me from errors of detail and led me to reconsider major themes in Latin American history. Emma Rothschild generously read one of the papers with a keen, cold eye; her comments were invaluable. I am greatly indebted to the Andrew W. Mellon Foundation, that wonderful benefactor of the humanities, for making the Atlantic History Seminar possible. Pat Denault has managed the Seminar in all its aspects with efficiency and grace. And I owe much to Ginger Hawkins, for her bibliographical assistance, her computer skills, and her bountiful good cheer. Most of all I thank the young historians to whom these pages are dedicated, who challenged me, and themselves, at every point.

Index